Four-Harness Weaving

by Kernochan Bowen

D1292627

WATSON-GUPTILL PUBLICATIONS/NEW YORK

Library of Congress Cataloging in Publication Data
Bowen, Kernochan.
  Four-harness weaving.
  Bibliography: p.
  Includes index.
  1. Hand weaving. I. Title.
TT848.B66 1978   746.1'4   78-88
ISBN 0-8230-1889-X

Manufactured in U.S.A.

First Printing, 1978

Contents

Preface

After reading prefaces all these years, I finally turned to the dictionary to see what they truly are. It told me a preface is, among other things, an explanation of the scope of the discourse.

Were I a real scholar, I would probably have continued on, to look up scope and discourse . . .

This book is designed to serve several functions. If you find yourself with a loom and threads, but no teacher, my hope is that it will enable you to start on the path to becoming a weaver. If you find yourself with the same equipment, still no teacher, but you have woven in some dim and dusty past period, this book should jog your memory and give you the confidence to take up weaving again. If you had a beginning weaving class at some point, but did not believe the teacher who advised you to take notes, then this book could substitute for the notes you didn't take. There are some important—or even crucial—steps in the weaving process that you won't want to miss when you take it up again.

The order in which processes are shown can present quite a problem. The subject—warping and weaving on a four-harness loom—is reminiscent of a small kitchen after a big party, when you simply cannot do the dishes until you get some dishes done.

For instance, I could have started with a list of terms used in weaving, but that is like the big party just mentioned where you are introduced to twenty-seven people in three minutes. Candidly, how many names did you recall—even before the first drink or canapé?

So I have not started with a big list, but instead have tried to introduce terms where they logically appear. Perhaps having photos with labeled parts of the loom will help those of you with orderly minds, but there is no requirement to learn the traditional names of all parts—only what they do, and how to adjust them so they will perform their respective jobs to your liking.

I am certainly no advocate of incorrect names, but will freely admit to having seen an impressive wall hanging come off the loom of a young lady who persisted in calling heddles ''those little jobbies with a round hook in the middle.'' I might not hire her to work as a clerk if I owned a hardware store, but weave she surely could.

My advice would be to read this book through with one of those transparent yellow markers in hand, the kind where you run over the line of type with the marker and the words suddenly stand out against a yellow background.

If you want to remember any particular section, point, or process, write the page and paragraph down in the back of the book. After all, this book is your own property, so there is nothing to prevent you modifying its form to make it more useful.

There will appear in this book, I am sure, some aspects of weaving that will be of little or no interest to you—now. Instead of ploughing through my deathless prose on these aspects, skim over them lightly. Weaving is not an assignment. It is not a course you must pass before you get into the next classroom. And, as it is presented here, it is a possible source of pleasure.

I had a student once who honestly tried to enjoy weaving. She came to my house on time, worked hard, asked intelligent questions, and was doing well in the technical details. I could see she was deriving no pleasure at all from the exercise, so I brought the conversation around to that.

She smiled beautifully, laid down her shuttle, and said perfectly pleasantly, "I hate weaving. I really do. It is no fun and I enjoy no part of it."

But before I could say anything, she added, "I haven't wasted my time or money though—not at all. I do a lot of traveling and museum visiting, and now I can really appreciate the care and skill that goes into weaving anything—even a skirt or a little wall hanging. It's been worthwhile, but I don't want to *do* it. I know that now."

Hallelujah, I thought. A very honest woman who is also wise. And that is what any craft or hobby is all about. You try it out, you explore it, you look at its various phases and faces, and if you end up not enjoying it, there should be no sense of guilt. At the very least, you have gained an appreciation of good workmanship and time spent by an artisan, and your taste has been refined.

I taught my daughter how to weave when she was twelve, because she asked me to. A few months later she confessed she didn't enjoy it much, and was much relieved when I told her that not only did she not have to enjoy it, she also didn't have to do it. "You know how," I said to her. "If you ever want to again, you won't have to take lessons. It's just another skill you have. You don't bake lemon pie every day. If you move to China, I suspect you won't do lemon pie even once a month. But you learned something when you had the chance—smart girl."

All this was to set the stage for giving you one piece of advice. Make enough short warps—a dozen or so—so you get the feel of the loom you are working on. If, after you are pretty competent at the pure mechanics of weaving, you still find no pleasure in the doing or the achieving, please don't feel bound to continue. Your pleasure may be in photography, growing perennials or at a potter's wheel.

A hobby is not a duty. And if we had more people who understood this, we might have fewer ghastly needlepoint pillows, and more fine pottery or even—hopefully—more happy weavers.

1.
Making a Sample Warp

A warp is the set of long threads that you put onto the loom before you start weaving, and that—when crossed with a weft—makes cloth.

A Sample Warp
Making a sample warp is basically the same as making any other warp. However, it is usually much narrower and much shorter than most warps you will make in the future. The smallest feasible warp is roughly 3" (8 cm) wide, and as long as it must be in order to weave a total of perhaps 6" (15 cm). This will probably work out to about a 20" (51 cm) warp on a table loom or a 30" (76 cm) warp on a floor loom.

These figures are, of course, minimum. Maximum can be very long or very wide. It is even possible to have different treadlings and threadings, and weft materials. The longer the warp the merrier, because more adventuring will then be possible.

The Warping Device
You will need a warping device for the warp making. In the photos we have used a warping frame rather than a warping mill because they are cheaper and more people can buy them.

Preparing the Yarns
Wind your yarn from the hank or the purchased ball into a new *loose* ball. This prevents the loss of the yarn's elasticity, and enables it to feed freely as you wind the warp. It also helps insure uniform tension of the warp, which is what we are after.

Cut a piece of yarn, in a different color than the warp colors, about 36" (91 cm) if you want a 30" (76 cm) warp or 26" (66 cm) if you want a 20" (51 cm) warp. Make a loop at each end. Try to find a non-stretchy yarn for this measuring cord. Make sure your cord, from end of loop to end of loop, measures at least the minimum you want. If not, cut another length of yarn that will.

Ends, Wefts, and Picks
The long threads on the loom, which are first arranged on the warping frame, are the warp ends. They are measured in ends per inch (epi). The threads crossing them on the loom are the wefts, which come across the warp ends in picks or rows.

How Many Ends Per Inch? And Why? This knitting worsted weight yarn is medium-coarse. You feel you want 10 ends per inch, but you are not quite sure. You might want 12—or you might even want 8 ends per inch.

Tradition says you are to strive for a 50/50 cloth, which is a cloth that has the same number of ends per inch as picks per inch. Surely you may vary this where, and by how much, you wish. But do try it out as an experiment just to see the resulting cloth.

Here we shall have 12 ends per inch for the first inch, 8 epi in the middle inch, and 10 epi for the last inch.

The reason for winding the inches of warp with the loosest inch in the middle is that, if the loose inch makes the little sample warp sleazy, it is preferable that this occur in the middle where it is kept moderately in line by the more dense outside inches.

Getting the Warp Started

Fit your measuring cord with loops at either end over four pegs (preferably in a horizontal or vertical row) of the warping frame.

Drop your loosely wound ball of wool into a bowl or something you can put on the floor. Slip knot the end of the ball to the first peg on the left, which you will call Peg A. Carry the yarn to the right, over Pegs B and C (the next two pegs) and down before Peg D.

Use one hand to wind while the other pulls yarn from the ball; that way you will get an even feed. Thus you will get an evenly wound warp and, believe me, you need an evenly wound warp.

The yarn is now down between Pegs C and D. Take it back around Peg D only once counterclockwise, and then back down to the left, between Pegs C and D. Continue by feeding it under Peg C and back over Pegs B and A.

You now have two warp ends wound since Peg A represents the front of the warp, and you have one yarn leading away from it, and one leading back to it.

A warping frame is a picture framelike square of wood, with dowels sticking out of it on the side facing the room not the wall.

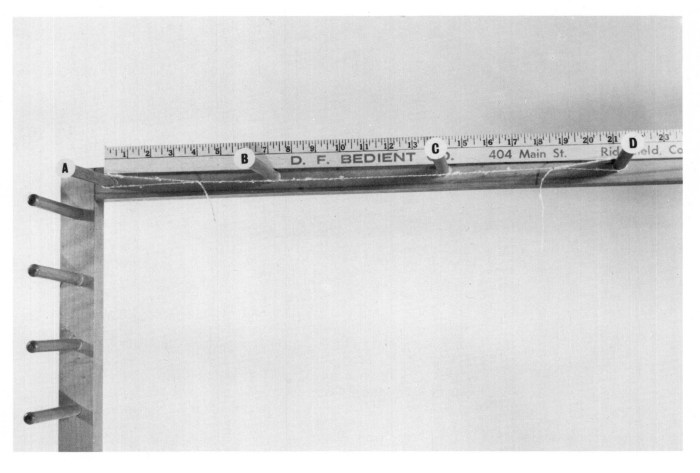

The Cross

As you repeat this series of motions—over B and C, under and around D, under C, over B, over and under A, and over B and C again, you will see a distinct cross form in the yarn between Pegs C and D. Every other thread goes upper left to lower right, and the alternate thread goes upper right to lower left.

Comfortably Continuing the Warp Winding

All your warps in the future will be made this way, so it is important to establish an easy and efficient procedure. Put the bowl in the exact spot most convenient for you. Set the warping frame at the height you want it. Sit on a chair that makes your back feel good.

Hang the warping frame on a wall at the right place for you, or set it on an upholstered bench at the angle you like.

I happen to prefer it set on our piano bench, pulled a little way out from the piano and tipped back against the keys. Then I sit on a little stool which has about 12" (30 cm) legs. But the whole setup suits me and that is the important thing.

Counting Ties Save Your Precious Time

Continue with the winding, A to D and back to A, A to D and back to A.

When you have wound 12 ends, or the first inch of warp, put on a counting tie to make life easier. If you do not (looking to the future when you may be making a 24" (61 cm) wide warp, with 32 ends per inch) you will be doing a lot of totally unnecessary counting.

Double a piece of yarn that contrasts in color with the warp; push the loop up behind the wound inch, in front of the wood frame, and at the cross. Reach down through the loop and pull up a new one, so the yarn goes around the warp inch you have just wound. This is easier if you use your other hand to maintain a degree of tension on the double ends.

Left
Label four horizontal pegs from left to right, A through D. Fit the piece of yarn with one loop over Peg A and the other over Peg D, enlarging or reducing the size of the loops to make a good fit, but being sure not to have a total length of less than the 30" (76.2 cm) or 20" (51 cm), whichever you have decided you want. If the pegs are too close together, change your Peg A to one that will give you the minimum required length.

Left
Tie the warp yarn around Peg A with a slip knot, taking the bight from the short end. Carry it over what we shall call the top (or north) surfaces of Pegs B and C. Then drop down to go around Peg D, counterclockwise, once. Now carry your yarn along so it touches the bottom (or south) side of Peg C, over the top (north) side of Peg B, and around Peg A counterclockwise, and back over the top surface of Peg B. You now have two warp ends wound, because Peg A is the front of the warp, and Peg D is the back of the warp.

Right
As you repeat this series of motions—over B and C, under and around D, under C, over B, over and under A, and over B and C again, you will see developing between Pegs C and D a distinct cross. Every other thread goes upper left to lower right, and the alternate thread goes upper right to lower left.

Left
Wind—do not tie—your yarn several times around Peg A to secure it, and then let it hang.

Below
Wind on a total of twelve ends—remember that is six loops at Peg D. Now mark the twelve ends off with a counting tie to indicate you have wound one inch of warp width.

A counting tie starts with a doubled length of yarn in a color contrasting with the warp.

Between Pegs C and D, at the cross, push the folded end of the tie-up—behind the warp, in front of the board itself. Now bring that folded yarn over the top of the wound warps. Reach down through the fold-loop and, with thumb and forefinger of one hand, while the other hand holds the ends of the tie, pull up a new fold-loop through the original one. This fold-loop will be made of the doubled yarn. Let it stay there.

Right
Wind on eight more warp ends—
that is, four more rounds at
Peg D.

Below
Now put your thumb and forefinger down through the new
loop, while holding the ends of
the tie to maintain some tension, and bring that loop down
over the bundle of the eight new
warp ends. Then pull through
it a new double loop, ready for
the next inch of warps.

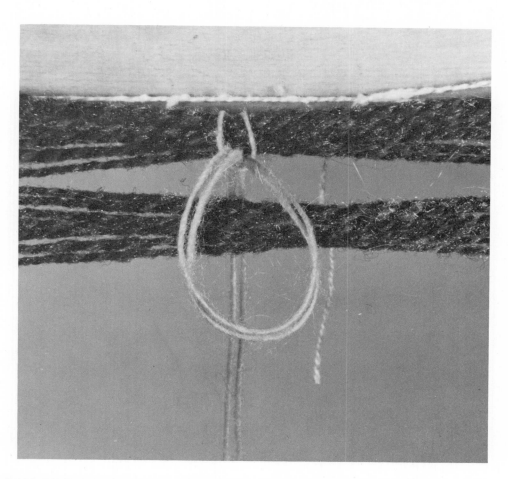

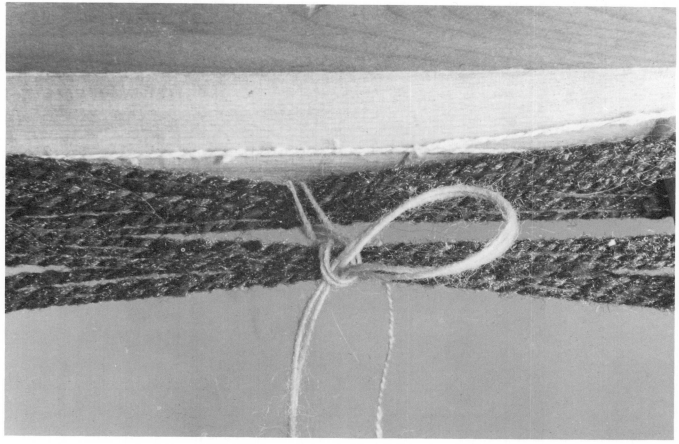

Above
Wind onto the frame ten more warp ends. At the front of the warp (Peg A) cut the warp yarn, leaving enough extra length so that you can tie a slip knot around that peg, and tighten it to make the tension of that warp end the same as the rest of the warp. Repeat the counting loop-tie and, while maintaining tension on the ends of the tie, pull up new loops through the old ones.

Left
This is the last inch of your warp, as you have decided it is to be 3" (8 cm) wide. That is why you repeated the looping sequence a few more times to lock the loops. The extra loops at the end have no warp bundle inside each loop, and will look like crocheting. Not to worry—that is what they really were all along.

Above
The cross is tied by poking the end of a length of yarn, in a color that contrasts with the color of the warp, to the right of Peg C, from the near side of the warp right to the wood of the frame. Now bring that same end from the wood frame back out to the near side of the warp again, but just to the left of Peg D. The actual cross in the yarn will be between the ends of the yarn. Tie the two ends together in a hard knot. I was told once that this is the only time in the weaving process when you tie a hard knot.

Right
Check to make very sure all the "up" threads of the cross are above the tie, and all the "down" threads of the cross are below it. Do this for both halves of the cross. If it proves not to be the case, unknot the yarn and do the operation over until all the up threads are up and all the down threads, for each half of the cross, are down.

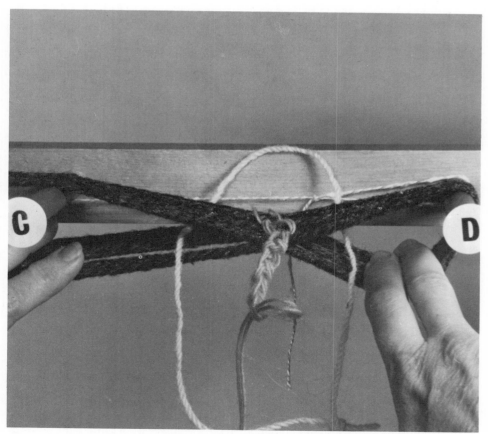

Let the new loop just hang there—although it will probably stand in a vertical fashion until you have wound the next inch. In this case, it will be the 8 ends inch. Repeat the looping procedure. And continue for each inch on every warp you ever wind. It is far easier to count the warp ends for only the 14th inch you have just wound than to count again for the preceding 13 as well.

It is indeed added insurance if, after the last planned inch of each warp (here it will be the 10 warps inch), you repeat the looping procedure a few times to prevent accidental unlooping.

It is true these loops will have no warps in them, but it will help insure that the yarn-enclosing loops will stay until you wish to pull out the whole counting tie.

Tie the Cross Tie the Cross Tie the Cross

After you have made your little sample warp, and before you take it off the frame, you must *tie the cross securely.*

This is the most important sentence in this book. Underline it. Star it in red at the margins. Do what you please, but make a mental note to remember it, even if you must forget your own name.

Cut a length of the contrasting color yarn. Push one end through to the left of the actual cross, which will be just to the right of Peg C. Pull it on through to the wood frame, and back out to the right of the actual cross, which will be just to the left of Peg D. Tie a tight knot, but leave space so the resulting loop is perhaps 6" (15 cm) in diameter.

The cross must be tied very securely because, if this is not done and you take the warp off the frame, you will lose the cross and not have a warp. You will have a mess of threads in no order whatsoever that will never make you a warp. You will have to throw the whole thing out and start again with new yarns.

Choke Ties

Some people prefer to tie choke ties (small cords used to keep your warp in order) every yard, but—particularly with a sticky or generally troublesome warp—I do believe that every half yard is more cheering to the heart and mind. For this warp, one choke tie is obviously the right number.

Check Before You Take the Warp Off the Board. Have you tied the cross? Check that first.

Do you have the number of inches wound which you decided was right? Count the little loops at the cross.

Are the choke ties tied? In other words does it look like a logical number for the length of the warp?

Take the Warp Off

If the warp is long enough to do so (which this one surely will not be), finger crochet it so it will unwind from the *back.* This action is just like the counting tie at the cross when you were winding the warp.

The only thing left to do is gloat. You have made a warp—a small and narrow one, true. But the system is the same whether you are making a warp for a single bookmark or to do upholstery for your favorite couch.

Congratulations.

With the warp still on the frame, tie a choke tie around the whole three inch bundle, between Pegs A and B. A choke tie is a piece of very strong yarn or cord, perhaps a shoelace, wrapped around the warp two or three times, and then tied with a slip knot.

Wrap and then make the first over and under as though you were tying your shoe. Lay the top end over the bottom one.

Pull a loop of that top yarn, made from the part beyond where it lies over the bottom one, into and out the old loop, while maintaining tension on the bottom yarn.

The directions are sometimes confusing, but don't be ashamed to reread them. And look at the photos carefully. Once you have this knot under control, you can show it to someone in about the length of time it takes to turn a page of a very large book. Make sure the tie is tight—*why do you suppose it is called a* choke tie?

2.
Figuring for a Warp

It would be reassuring, when you have a project in mind and the threads in front of you, to know you have enough material to make the project. Of course, if you bought cones, spools, or hanks that had the size of the yarn, the yards per pound (or the meters per kilo) and the weight printed on them somewhere, then there is no problem if you know how to figure how many yards you will need.

Let us run through that simple little mathematical computation to make sure this first and easy step is well understood.

Ends Per Inch
You know that you will need 16 warp ends per inch (epi) because you decided that *after you had done your sample.* The traditional ideal is to have the same number of warps per inch as wefts. The warps are the long threads you put on the loom. The wefts are what you cross the warps with—and these threads usually are wound on shuttles of some variety.

Total Number of Ends. If your project warp is to be 14" (35 cm) wide, and 5½ yards (5 m) long, then multiply 16 times 14 to give you the total number of ends you will need. That is, the ends in one inch of warp width are multiplied by the actual warp width. Hopefully, you and I will agree that the answer is 224 ends. If you can visualize 224 ends that are each 5½ yards (5 m) long, we can move to the next stage.

The Total Length of Warp
Your project is to be less than 5 yards (4½ m) long when taken off the loom. The 5½ yard (5 m) warp length figure comes because there will be (on the mythical loom you are using) about 25" (63 cm) of waste. About 20" (51 cm) of that warp will be at the back.

How to Figure Back Wastage. The back wastage figure—for any loom—is the distance from where you can no longer weave the warp to the actual end of that warp. It will be roughly the same on any given loom, regardless of the warp width, length, or material.

You will no longer be able to weave because the back end of the warp comes closer and closer to the harnesses as it is woven and then advanced. (Harnesses are the picture frame-like devices that hold the heddles. Heddles are the metal needles with the eye in the middle.) This makes it increasingly difficult to raise the harnesses as they are being held down by the advancing bar—the one over which the warps were looped.

Weave until you can no longer comfortably get a shed—the space through which you put the shuttle to lay in a pick of weft (A pick is the weaving term for a row).

The measurement from fell line—where the cloth becomes warp at the front of the loom—to the actual end of the warp is back wastage.

How to Figure Front Wastage. The knots that you tied at the front before you started weaving cannot be woven, so they are called front wastage.

How to Figure Total Wastage. The sum of the two figures plus take-up is warp wastage. There is more back and front wastage on a big deep floor loom than on a small compact table loom.

Also there will be take-up while weaving. You should bubble heavy weft to make it not pull in at the selvedges. This is done by laying in very heavy weft so it looks like scallops, with the points toward you, before it is beaten. It is fairly obvious there is weft take-up in this case, but it is not immediately obvious there must be warp take-up as well. On your notes for a project, figure what take-up amounted to with different threads, patterns, and beats. Eventually you will come up with an individual figure for types of yarns and weaves. Until then why not use 10% for everything? I think you will be reasonably safe with that.

Back to the arithmetic—multiply 224 by 5½. We will need 1,232 yards (1,126½ m) 224 ends, each of which is 5½ yards (5 m) long.

How to Manage with Insufficient Warp

Supposing you have only 1,200 yards (1,097 m) and great determination. You can make your project a fraction narrower, if you feel the width is negotiable—e.g., tote bags you have designed. Remember each end is 5½ yards (5 m) long. You don't have to leave off many ends to save 32 yards (29 m).

But supposing you have great determination, have centered your pattern (on graph paper) on the warp, and have the wisdom to know your 14" (35 cm) warp is the minimum width you require—perhaps you feel the length could be negotiable.

You have allowed a traditional 25" (63 cm) for warp waste. But since you have used this loom before, you know that 18" (46 cm) in the back is enough, and you can carefully get by with 4" (10 cm) in the front where you are tying on. That only gives you 672" (1,705 cm) of saved warp, which is over 18 yards (16½ m). Now will you admit you better make it a bit narrower?

Checking Your Arithmetic

If you are measuring your warp in inches, remember to divide by 36 to get your final answer in yards. For example, 16 epi, 14" (36 cm) wide, 78" (198 cm) long warp. 16 times 14 is 224 ends. 224 times 78 is 17,472 inches (44,379 cm) not yards. To get yards, we must divide the 17,472 by 36, which should give 485⅓ yards (444 m).

Similarly, should your warp length be figured in feet? Then remember to divide the answer from ''ends per inch times width of warp, times foot length of warp'' by three, to give total yards needed.

Figure Out and Write Down Yarn Yardages

It is a good thing to keep a little section of your weaving notebook with notations of the yardages per pound of yarns you use often. For instance, if you know how many yards are in Shetland wool—the brand you like—or baby wool by a certain manufacturer, then you can very quickly tell how much you need for a project.

The old weaving books said to allow a few extra ounces—a half pound according to some books. I do wonder whether they would have said that if they knew today's yarn prices. I think not.

If you have a postal scale around the house, you can reel off an ounce of something, and then measure it to find the number of yards per ounce. For thrift's sake, do not measure as a friend of mine once did. She wound around a huge heavy clip, and thus considerably lowered her estimate of yardage per pound.

What if you have no postal scale? Well, you can get a rough idea of yards per ball by winding a whole one around the longest flat shuttle you can find. Multiply the inch length of the shuttle by two, and then multiply that figure by the number of threads going around the shuttle. Divide by 36, and you should have approximately the number of yards to that ball.

If you are fortunate enough to have a niddy noddy (a tool used for forming skeins), wind your ball onto that, tie the hank in three places before you remove it, and then figure the total yardage. Do that by measuring the hank's open center, multiplying by two for one round; and multiply that by the number of threads in the hank. To get yards per hank, remember to divide by 36 here too.

Don't Let Numbers Numb You

I think we would all be more comfortable with this mathematical aspect of weaving if we realized it is about third or fourth grade level. It is not algebra—it is not calculus—and was being done thousands of years before scratch pads and ball-point pens were even thought of. Relax.

3.
Putting a Warp on the Loom

Traditionally this procedure is known as beaming the warp. This chapter will cover a range of steps from holding a chained warp in your hands to the stage when you are ready to thread the heddles.

Remember the cross that was tied very carefully before taking the warp off the warping board? You are now going to use it. Find the place where the cross is tied—it will be quite close to the back of the warp. The back is what will come unchained first because any warp is chained from front to back.

Lay the warp on something flat. A table is ideal, but a reasonably clean floor—even a bed, couch, or chair—will do.

Inserting the Lease Sticks

With your loom you have a pair of lease sticks. They are slightly longer than the maximum width it is possible to weave on that loom. At the end of each stick is a drilled hole through which cords or shoelaces go.

Put one lease stick through the path prepared for it by the string tying the cross, that is, half the lease, leash, or cross. All three names are acceptable. Now repeat the procedure with the other lease stick through the other half of the lease.

Tie the lease sticks together at their ends and allow an inch or so in between them to insure that the threads will run over easily. Shoelaces can also be used for this step.

Look through the warp along the path on which one lease stick goes. Are all the threads above the string *above* the lease stick? Are all the threads below the string *below* the lease stick?

If this is not the case, untie the lease sticks and redo the steps in the previous paragraphs.

After the lease sticks are tied, you will see that they duplicate the path made by the string. This means you may take out the string. But be absolutely sure the lease sticks are securely tied. And do not remove the lease sticks until after the warp ends are tied on at the front of the loom.

"Only after I've tied each bout,
May those darned lease sticks come out."

"Lease sticks in
Till weavings begin."

Terrible poetry, but it may help you recall this part of the procedure. Not only are there no directions in this book to help you with the ensuing difficulties that forgetfulness will cause, but I know of no directions in any book.

Attaching the Raddle to the Back Beam

There are many ways of beaming a warp. No way is right—or wrong. The right one for you is the method that makes your success the easiest.

The method that works best for me is with a raddle firmly held to the top of the back beam. A raddle can be a board into which nails are pounded every inch, starting ½" (1.3 cm) out from the center, at each side of the center. The raddles appearing on the floor looms in this book are made of 3½" (9 cm) long dowels, which have been fitted into pre-drilled holes in a 1"×1½" (2.5 cm × 4 cm) board—whose length is the length of the back beam. The dowel at the center point is put out of line so we will know it is the center point, without having to check.

Because a raddle centered on the back beam is crucial as well as difficult to maintain when the raddle is tied to the back beam, a hole can be drilled at either end of the back beam and a matching hole at either end of the raddle. Two big nails that fit the holes are filed smooth on the ends. Dropped right down, they hold the raddle steady during the beaming process.

Obviously you cannot drill holes in other people's looms if you are in a class and are not using your own loom, so you must tie the raddle on. Be sure you tie it very securely; hooking it on with rubber bands is an even better idea.

Tying the Lease Sticks at Heddle-Eye Height

Now tie the lease sticks to some part of the castle, the framework that encloses the harnesses. Do this at whatever point works best for the loom you are using—at about heddle-eye height—which means at each end of the castle, probably through the shoelaces you used to tie the lease sticks together.

Flip the warp chain over the tops of the harnesses or over the top castle, and toward the front of the loom. If your warp is narrow enough, you could shove the heddles back on either side of center and put the chain through the resulting space.

Looking directly down at the lease sticks, you will see that every other warp end goes over one stick and under the next. Also the next thread over in either direction does exactly the opposite, under one stick and over the next. The threads are in order and you may proceed to the next step.

Slipping the End Loops Over the Dowel

Now look at those counting ties you made as you were winding the warp. Each loop clasps an inch of warp. Separate the last tied inch slightly from the rest of the warp. Lay a finger on top of the lease stick closer to the back beam, but under the inch of warp ends riding on that lease stick.

Slide your finger toward the back beam, and you will find an inch of warp looped around your finger. If you don't believe me, count the warp loops on your finger. Should your warp be planned for 10 epi, you will have 5 loops; since each loop equals two ends, you have your 10 epi right there. A warp planned for 5 epi means two loops on one dowel, three on the next. This is because two loops are four ends, and

Lease sticks are put through the warp at the cross. One stick is put carefully through one half of the cross, and the second is put—with equal care—through the other half. Tie the sticks together at both ends securely, with at least an inch (2.5 cm) between them.

Check the placement of the lease sticks. Do they exactly duplicate the yarn cross? If not, untie them and try again until they do.

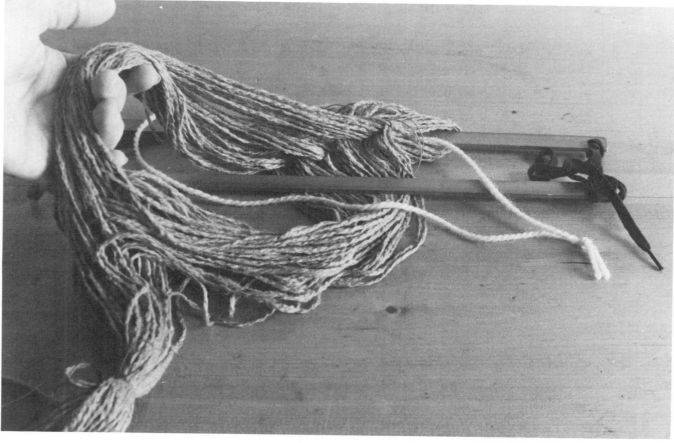

Get that raddle centered on the back beam by tying it on, or hooking it on with heavy rubber bands. Don't use masking tape because it makes the back beam, the raddle, and the warp sticky.

Lease sticks are now tied to a handy part of the castle, at heddle eye height, to make the next steps easier.

Look at any warp thread, and it will be going over one lease stick and under the next one. Check the warp to its left and the warp to its right. Both will be doing the opposite, going under where the middle one went over, and going over where the middle one went under.

three loops are six ends, six and four is ten, for 2″ (5 cm), so it will turn out to be 5 epi.

Drop that 1″ (2.5 cm) wide loop over a dowel of the raddle.

If your warp is to be say 22″ (60 cm) wide, remember to loop over the peg marked 10½″ (27 cm). If you will put your outside inch at the 10½″ (27 cm) point, half your warp inch will be toward the center and half toward the selvedge. 10½ plus ½ is 11, so your warp will roll on at 22″ (60 cm) wide as you planned and wound it.

Continue to the End of the Warp. Go straight across the pegs this way—skipping the center peg if your warp is an even number of inches in width.

With an uneven number of inches in the warp, you do use the middle peg—purely because that is the only way I can get the warp wound on at roughly the predetermined width, without it being uneven at one side. In this case, you start one peg in from what seems reasonable. Example: a 5″ (13 cm) warp would be hooked over the 1½, ½, center, ½, and 1½ pegs, for a total width of 4″ (10 cm) on the raddle. But it would be evenly spaced on the raddle—and when correctly sleyed would return to its five-inch width.

Protecting Your Arrangement

You now have an inch of warp on each one of the pegs. Take rubber bands, yarn, or string and pop over the tops of the pegs, so the warp ends do not bounce off when you snap the warp sharply—and you will.

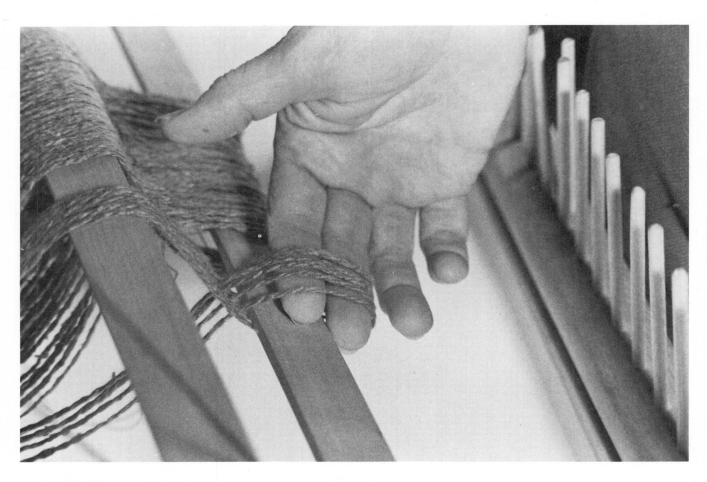

To get the inch of the warp width you tied last anchored to the raddle, do the following—slowly. Slightly separate that inch from its fellow inches by putting a finger over the near lease stick and under the warps. Slide your finger back to the raddle and the back beam. There is your inch of warp, tied at the front by the counting ties (out of the photo), and ready to be put over a dowel.

Drop the inch of warp loops over the correct dowel. In this case, it will be on the dowel 12th to the left—or right—of center, because the warp is 25" (63.5 cm) wide. Go straight across the warp and raddle in the same fashion, making sure the inches are "turned" in the same direction. The direction does not matter, but it must be consistent.

Slipping in the Bar

Then take a bar, a very heavy dowel, a mop handle, or any of these at least a couple of inches longer than the warp is wide. On most of my looms, ½" (1.3 cm) brass plated rods, *not hollow*, are cut so long they will only just roll onto the warp beams.

Poke the rod through each inch of warp loops at the back of the raddle, to the middle of the warp. Go either up or down according to your fancy, but be consistent all across the warp.

You now have half the warp ends attached to the bar, but the bar is not attached to the loom.

Attaching the Bar to the Back Apron

Go back to your warping frame. Using strong plied cord (that you have probably bought from the hardware store) make three loops of exactly the same size on the warping frame. They will be the same size if you use two of the pegs in the manner shown in the photo—a procedure we shall repeat later on for string heddles.

Snitch one of the loops to the back bar of the loom, the one that *is* attached to the warp beam. Then snitch it to the bar that is *not* attached to the loom—the one with warp ends looped over it. Repeat the procedure with the next loop, having first centered it on the bar attached to the loom. Now slide the other half of the warp inches onto the bar. Then snitch your third and last cord loop to both bars.

Because you have approximately equalized the pressures—toward the back because of the drag from the brake assembly, and toward the front because of the drag from the person holding the warp there—you should have no problems.

Winding On the Warp

Snap the warp at the front so the threads lie flat and in order. If you will do this while holding on at a choke tie, I think you will be delighted with how well it works.

Roll a complete round of warp onto the warp beam. Check to be sure the brass bar and the loom bar are equally parallel to the warp beam. They should be; if they are not, unwind that round, adjust the bars to a parallel position, and wind your round again.

Winding in Sticks each Round. Now comes another controversy. Shall you wind in sticks, paper, plastic, cardboard, or just what? Some people wind in rolls of wrapping paper, some use sticks, some prefer pre-cut sheets of plastic, and some use great rolls of cardboard.

I am a stick or a newspaper person myself. A dozen lathes, cut long enough so that they will only just roll onto the warp beam, solve my problems in this area. A few strokes with a block of sandpaper on the lathes are helpful, then an application of a bit of floor wax, considering the quality of wood today.

The reason for rolling anything at all into the warp as you crank to roll it on around the beam is to keep threads from cutting through to the center. Have you ever tried to snap off a bit from a card wound with yarn? Sometimes the wool is stouter than you think it is, and the end cuts right past its fellow yarns and disappears—probably forever. That is why something must be wound into the warp. If you do it after every round, you will run into no difficulty. No warp ends are much longer because they have cut their way through to the center.

Lay a stick in after the first round of cranking and go to the front of the loom.

Rubber bands, or string, are now affixed to the dowels, above the warp inches, to keep the warps from leaping off during later stages of the warping.

The warp is attached to a rod by poking that rod through the warp ends loops, behind the raddle. (A stick has been substituted in the photo to make this process more clear, but the rod will go back in after this photo.) Note that the loops are again "turned" in the same direction.

For me, the two-people approach is the easiest. Two people does not necessarily mean two weavers; it means two live bodies and one is you, the weaver. I would rather have the other person at the back and cranking on while I hold the warp in front of the loom. When you say to, the person will crank, will stop, and will lay in a stick.

Spreading and Evening the Warp. During this time, you are at the front of the loom holding the warp at a moderate degree of tension so it winds on firmly, and you are spreading it out as wide as you can with your two hands. Sometimes it helps to run the warp under the cloth beam, then up and down over the breast beam, because that will keep the warp spread out better than your hands can do.

Make three separate loops the same size, of nylon cord—or something very strong indeed—on the warping frame. Using the two pegs as a "jig" insures the three loops will be the same size.

Snitch the first loop to the loom's back bar or rod at A, and then to the extra rod on which you have half the inches of warp. Snitch the center loop at B, as you did at A. Put on the rest of the warps as you did the first half, and finish by snitching the third loop to the loom at the other edge of the warp.

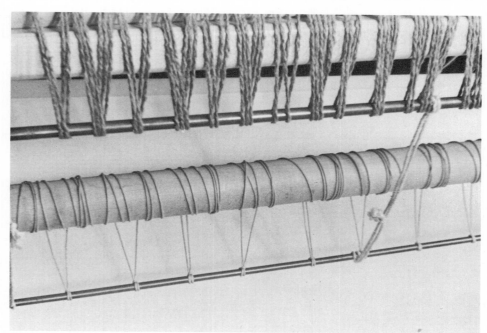

Use Those Choke Ties. Every time a choke tie comes to the breast beam, untie it and snap the warp, and spread carefully again. Because the ties appear at fairly regular intervals, the warp will probably be snapped and spread often enough to keep it even.

Crank on a round, lay in a stick, crank on another round, and pull the warp evenly taut. On a wide warp you may have to do that by pulling the warp in sections, a few inches on the selvedge, a few more inches, and so on, right across the warp.

What you are trying to achieve is a warp wound onto that warp beam evenly and closely—not tight, not loose, not even half way in-between. A firm even warp is the goal, and everything helps including the placement of the choke ties.

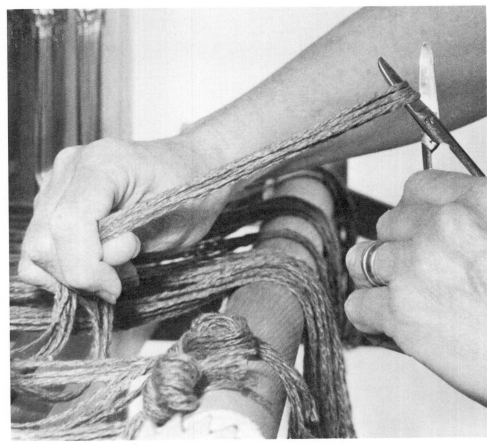

Winding On a Warp: Different Approaches

There is a lot of argument about the methods of winding on a warp. The thing to strive for is the one that works best for you.

There are: the tension versus no tension, the two people versus one person, the do-it-all-from-the-front-so-no-raddle school, the take-out-the-harnesses-and-run-the-warp-over-(or under)-the-breast-beam crew. In other words this matter has not been totally settled for all time and for all weavers. My advice to you is to try out all methods you hear about and quietly decide for yourself.

This system works for me and all I can do is recommend it. Keep on cranking and laying in sticks until the warp is wound on—that is, until no more warp is left beyond a few inches lying in front of the harnesses.

Another method may work better for you.

Don't Wind On the Last Few Inches. Those inches will be needed, so don't wind them on. And if you have, just release the back brake for a turn or a half turn, and pull your needed few inches toward the front again.

Cut and Slip Knot the Loops. You will now have loops at the front of the loom—doubled ends we might also call them. Take a group about an inch in width and pull taut. Cut with sharp scissors at the very end of the loops.

Be sure to slip knot these ends immediately, taking the bight from the short end. If you forget this, you have a fair chance of losing warp ends from the lease sticks whether someone lays a coat on the warp, or the cat decides to investigate this new plaything. Continue cutting and slip knotting across the warp.

You Can Put On a Warp

For a narrow warp or on a small (floor or table) loom, you can put on a warp by yourself. And when you have done it a few times, you will surely try out a wider one—and successfully too.

There now, you have made and beamed a warp.

If you run the warp from the raddle on the back beam (A), over the warp beam (which is not visible), under the cloth beam (B), then up and down over the breast beam (D), some people feel it is easier to spread the warp. In this photo, all the harnesses, and the reed and top member of the beater as well, have been removed, leaving the bottom member only (C). The lease sticks are still in of course, and one shows faintly between back beam (A) and cloth beam (B).

The last few inches of your warp length are now lying in front of the harnesses, and over the cloth beam in this case. Pull a small group even and taut with your fingers; then cut it at the end of the loops. Be sure to slip knot these ends immediately. And take the bight from the short end. This is to prevent "losing the cross," which might happen if someone laid a coat over the warp on a floor loom—or if your cat checks out this new acquisition. Cut and slip knot the ends right on across the warp.

4.
Threading

Before you thread your loom, it would be nice to know you had enough heddles on the right harnesses. If you discover in the midst of threading that you do not, then extra string heddles must be tied, which is easy but annoyingly time consuming.

How Many Heddles Are Needed
The simplest way to find out how many heddles are on each harness is to count them. But this matter is something like telling time; you don't really care what time it is—or how many heddles. What you want to know is how long before the bus is due in, or are there enough heddles for what you want to do? If we agree on this, count the heddles on harness one, then count half the heddles on harness 1, and put a bright little tie of yarn into the top of the middle heddle. Do this for all the harnesses—putting one color on harnesses 2 and 4 and a contrasting color on harnesses 1 and 3. This may reduce the chance of a threading error for you; I know it does for me.

Now let us assume the following: your threading pattern is 1 2 1 4 3 4. This means several things. A threading unit is six threads, or ends. Also, on harness 1 there will be—in one unit—two ends; on harness 2—in one unit—one end; on harness 3—in one unit—one end; and two ends on harness 4—in one unit, to each unit, whichever phrase makes the matter clearer to you.

Perhaps we could write it out so:

Harnesses	Ends
1	2
2	1
3	1
4	2

When we add the numbers in the Ends column we come up with six, which is correct because there are six threads in a threading unit. The wound warp we shall say is 180 ends.

Now, 180 divided by 6 gives 30. That 30 means we will have 30 threading units across the warp, so we can go back to our little figures and say:

Harnesses				Ends
1	equals	2×30	=	60
2	equals	1×30	=	30
3	equals	1×30	=	30
4	equals	2×30	=	60
				180

When we add the number of threads on all the harnesses we get 180, which is the total number of ends in the warp. So far so good.

How To See That They Are There. Now we want to know how many threads must be on each harness: to the right of the center for right-handed weavers, and to the left of the center for left-handed weavers. We might put it this way:

Harnesses					Ends
1	equals	$2 \times 30 = 60$	divided by 2	=	30
2	equals	$1 \times 30 = 30$	divided by 2	=	15
3	equals	$1 \times 30 = 30$	divided by 2	=	15
4	equals	$2 \times 30 = 60$	divided by 2	=	30
					90

When we add up the last column, we know that 90 is half of 180 and that two halves make a whole; life is satisfactory indeed.

Now go to the loom. Count 30 heddles to the right of the center (to the left if you are left-handed) on harness 1, and slide them way over to the left (to the right if you are left-handed). Do the counting and sliding for the other harnesses.

To keep the remaining heddles out of your way—those on the right which you won't be using (on the left if you are left-handed)—you could loosely tie a shoelace or something around them and the side castle of the loom. Or run a yardstick through to their immediate left, until you get some heddles threaded. They themselves will become the markers.

You have already tied the lease sticks with string at either end to some part of the castle, and you have tied them at a height approximately level with the heddle eyes while threading the heddles. The next step of raising the harnesses will lower the warp somewhat, which I find the perfect position to make heddle threading easy. If you have not achieved this, retie the lease sticks to a height that does please you.

Raising the Harnesses of a Rising Shed Loom
Most people find it easier to thread a loom if the harnesses are raised temporarily, and various rising shed looms have different ways of doing this. You can step on enough treadles so all the harnesses are up at once, but your ankles will tire eventually. You can, on a loom

with convenient top castle, tie a cord around that and through the tops of the harnesses. One of my looms has a system in which you step on the treadles to raise them and shoot a long heavy pin through pre-drilled holes right through the castle and through the tops of the harnesses as well.

If you are too lazy to do any of these (and there is nothing wrong with being lazy in the right places and at the right times), often you may remove the reed from the batten or remove the batten (beater) itself. Or you may reverse the problem and solve it that way.

Or Lower Yourself. In other words, don't raise the harnesses, just lower yourself. Sit on a very low chair or a small stool and thread from that position.

Once I took a workshop in a craft center where some construction work was being done. A borrowed cement block from the yard proved to be precisely the correct height for threading the antique loom I had been assigned. The important point here is to be comfortable.

A lot of sinking shed looms have a removable breast beam. Usually you bang it upward and it will come off because it is a press fit. Again you use a low chair or stool and thread from that position. Also remove the reed, which makes threading even easier.

Some loom makers' products have beaters and breast beam assemblies that lie down on the floor in front of the loom if the right bolts are undone.

The Actual Method of Threading

Sit down at the loom with your threading plan either tacked or taped to the loom, and reach through the tangle of heddles back to the lease sticks. The warp ends will be hanging in front of the harnesses waiting to be threaded. This is why you tied the extra heddles loosely to the right—so they wouldn't get mixed up with the heddles you are about to use.

Take the group of threads farthest to the right on the lease sticks, untie it, and hold the threads taut with your right hand. Now pick off the first four threads—going from right to left—with the fingers of your left hand, so they are placed in the four spaces between your four fingers and thumb. Be very sure you do this step to the left of some of the heddles you are about to use.

Number one end is the most right-hand end on those lease sticks, and it comes between your thumb and forefinger. The next three ends appear, in order, in the remaining three spaces between your four fingers.

Next step is to choose a heddle to thread the first end into. If your threading pattern is 1 2 1 4 3 4, the first end must go into harness 4, or harness 1 if you are left-handed.

Remember, we want to have the units appear like this: 1 2 1 4 3 4 and you are threading right to left (or left to right if you are left-handed.)

With the little finger of your right hand, while still holding the four threads in order with your left hand, hook around the most right-hand heddle on harness 4. Slide the right little finger down the heddle to about the eye of it. Holding the four ends with a bit of tension to make this step easier, take the first end with your right thumb and forefinger from between your left thumb and forefinger. Use a rolling motion with your right thumb and first two fingers, which permits you to fold

With your right hand, take a small group of threads and hold them reasonably taut.

Using the fingers of your left hand, pick off in order the first four threads, which will then appear in the four spaces between your five fingers. Check to be certain this is all happening to the left of the heddles you will be using next.

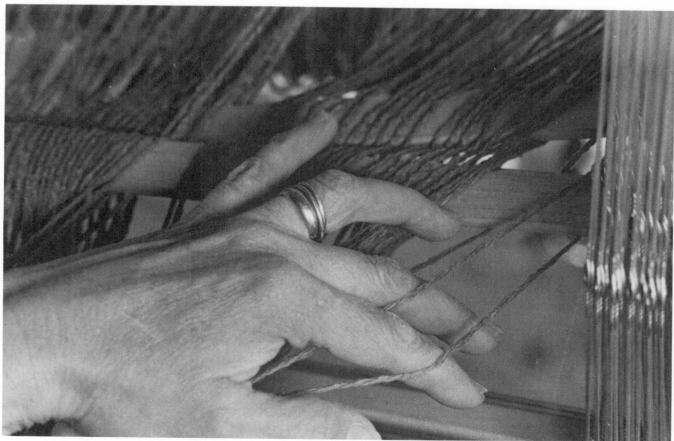

the end over and thread the eye of the heddle as though you were threading a needle. Actually this is precisely what you are doing. The eye of the needle just happens to be in its middle, not at one end.

Pull the end through the heddle eye completely, so the cut end of the yarn lies in front of the harnesses and hangs down a couple of inches.

There is a good reason for this. If you have extra length, you are not as likely to cross one end behind another heddle, which produces crossed heddles that you would have to straighten out later on. If no extra length has been left, loosen the back brake for half a round or so, as suggested in the last chapter.

By now you have surely figured out the goal here—there must be a straight feed from back roller to front roller; over lease sticks in order, tied on in order, and rolled over the breast beam onto the cloth roller —still in order.

Now take the end which is between your first two fingers, choose the most right-hand heddle on harness 3 and thread it in the same fashion as you did the previous end.

When you have finished the first four ends, you will have two ends left to complete the unit. Pick them off the cross just as you did the first four; thread through a heddle on harness 2 for the next to the last and last one going on harness 1.

When you have threaded a couple of threading units (about a dozen ends) slip knot them together in front of the harnesses, taking the bight from the *short* end; this way the knot and threaded ends will not pull out if the cat jumps up on the lease sticks at the back of the loom.

Left
The absolute right-hand end should now be between your left thumb and forefinger. The next three ends are in the three spaces between your four fingers, in order.

Bottom Left
Using the little finger of your right hand, hook it around the most right-hand heddle on harness 4. (The left hand can't help because it should still be holding the four threads in order!)

Right
If you hold the four ends slightly taut, it will be easier to take the first end from that group with your right thumb and first two fingers.

You'll want to do this with a "roll," so you can fold the end and thread it through the heddle eye in one motion. It is simply threading a needle whose eye is in its middle, not at one end.

Finish pulling that end through, so the cut end lies in front of the harnesses, hanging down for a few inches. The photo shows four ends threaded and hanging down, waiting to be slip knotted. If you look carefully, you can see they have been threaded from the lease sticks in order.

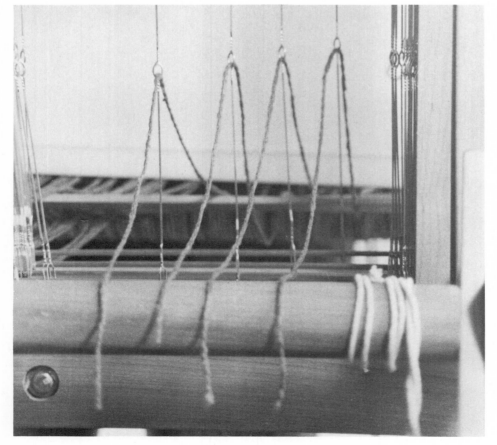

When you have threaded roughly an inch—or enough groups to make an inch, don't bother to count, just guess—slip knot that group. Take the bight from the short end, or any pressure will untie the knot.

In this photo there are extra unused heddles between each threading unit and the next one. The unit was eight and there are eight empty heddles before the next unit. This is a clever way to get out of taking heddles off harnesses when you have a wide warp, to be sleyed at a few ends per inch. Given that situation, you would use so few heddles that the surplus would rub and chafe the selvedge ends if you didn't do something to prevent it. But do be sure to figure the extra heddles in when you are doing the heddle figuring.

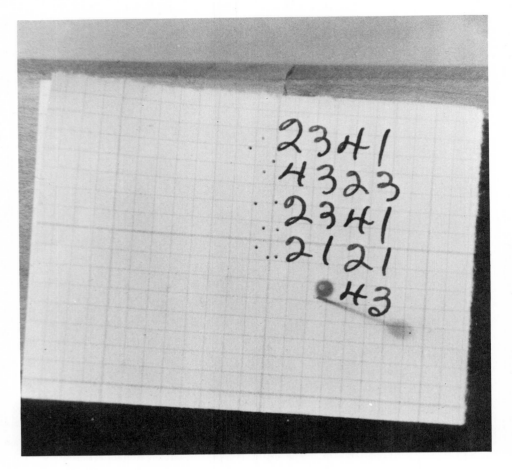

I slip knot by units usually, but habit is the only advantage I can cite.

This is an unbelievably slow way to thread heddles—to start with. The only analogy I can give you is touch typing versus hunt and peck. However, I strongly urge you to try this method for three months. If by then you've figured out a quicker way, write me a letter. Past teaching experience tells me you will then probably be threading at a rate of 300 heddles an hour in any pattern you are likely to try. And that is not bad!

When we get to the sleying, a slight variation on this system will do that job at a similarly speedy rate.

When Interruption Strikes

Before threading, write the unit—by fours—on a card and attach the card to the loom. If you have a threading unit of, say, 28 threads, write out the first four threads on one line, the next four on the next line, and so forth. Read the card from the right if you are right-handed.

If the telephone rings, you are likely to finish the four threads you have in your left hand. Then stick a pin on the line of numbers corresponding to the just finished four ends, and you will know where to begin again—in five minutes or a week from the interruption.

5.
Sleying

This is the step in weaving that largely determines the density of the Finished cloth. Will it be a stout commercial grade upholstery, or a gauzy summer baby blanket? The first part of this decision was choosing warp threads, then the pattern, and now the sett or the number of ends per inch.

If you wanted a sett of 8 epi in an 8D (dent, or the space between the metal uprights) reed, you would sley it singly. If you wanted a sett of 8 epi in a 6D reed, you would sley 1-1-2. A sett of 24 epi in a 12D reed would be sleyed 2-2-2. It isn't really so confusing, when you stop to think about it.

Reeds Are . . .

Reeds come in two metals these days—stainless steel and *non*-stainless steel. The stainless is a lot more expensive, but if you live by the seaside or in another area of high humidity, you don't have much choice.

Originally reeds were just that—splits of reed placed upright between a pair of horizontal sticks. The splits had to be held firmly in their assigned positions. Because precise measuring devices had not yet been invented, a plied cord was wound tightly around each of the horizontal sticks. If cords were the same size for their entire lengths and were wound closely, you then got even spaces between the wraps into which you glued the splits.

The above paragraph is not only an interesting historical note, but was inserted here to make sure you understand why reeds must be kept in good order. If primitive weavers went to all that trouble, we would probably do well to emulate them.

A reed that has been bent out of shape—even for a couple of dents —is about as much good as a plastic measuring cup warped from standing too close to the heat. If you persist in using a reed like this, you will have a streak running the length of the cloth. A reed determines the density of the cloth and will continue to do so—even when some parts are not uniform with the rest.

Now to get to the actual sleying. One of several tools could be used to put the threaded ends through the reed. One tool is a threading hook, which is a device that resembles a flattened crochet hook. Or you could use a dull-edged dinner knife, or a reed hook, which is also called an S hook because it has the appearance of a very fat S.

Should you have a 36″ (91 cm) wide loom and a 14″ (35 cm) wide warp, you will need to get that warp absolutely centered in the reed because any warp should be centered on any size loom. Since your goal is to have a completely straight line for each warp thread, you should check your warp at all points—when the warp is initially wound on, then through the winding on process, the lease sticks, the heddles, and now the reed, and later when it is tied on, and still later woven off.

Center the Reed in the Beater

With a ruler or tape measure, find the true center of the reed and tie a bit of bright yarn there permanently. Again with a ruler or tape, find the absolute center of the beater and put a mark on the shuttle race. The shuttle race is the shelf-like projection toward the weaver that is just below the bottom of the reed on the beater. Sometimes the marks do not line up on a new (or old) loom. Loosen the reed in the beater. This is done by some device the loom maker has used, most likely a couple of wing nuts. Loosen them enough so you can slide the reed back and forth, to line up the mark and the tie of yarn. Then tighten the wing nuts or whatever, so the reed won't slide any more.

If it still slides, you can cut up a couple of rubber bands into small enough pieces so they will lie flat in the bottom of the trough made for the bottom of the reed. The friction between the reed bottom and the rubber usually solves the problem nicely.

You have a 36″ (91 cm) wide reed in this imaginary loom and a 14″ (35 cm) warp to be centered in it. Take half the warp width figure and (if you are right-handed) lay in a bit of yarn in the dent that is 7″ (18 cm) to the right of center. If you are a real perfectionist, count dents to see whether you have measured correctly. For example, with an 8D reed, count 8 × 7 and that will be 56 dents from center.

Your ends now are tied in groups at the front of the heddles because the threading process is finished.

There is a gadget you can buy to snap over the beater and breast beam in order to keep the beater from flopping back and forth while sleying; however, it doesn't seem to be necessary for me after the first couple of bunches are pulled through and slip knotted. I would rather spend that money on threads.

The Method of Sleying

If you are right-handed, you must shove all those bunches of slip knotted ends over a little to the left. Untie the most right-hand group. Holding the bunch of ends in your right hand with slight tension to make picking easier, pick with the fingers of your left hand the first four ends. This is done in the spaces between your five fingers, exactly as when you threaded.

Take up the reed hook in your right hand and slide it through the reed, front to back, at the place where you put the yarn—7″ (18 cm) to the right of center.

Hook the end that is the most right-hand one of the warp, which is lying between your left thumb and forefinger, and pull it through the reed. You should have enough extra length so it can lie over the shuttle race a few inches, and thus be less likely to pull out of the reed.

This is an 8D reed and you want an 8 epi sett. You have four ends in your left hand, so when they are sleyed you will have sleyed half an inch. If you slip knot the ends in front of the reed, with the beater at a

Hook through the reed to the most right-hand warp end, with the hook in your right hand. Pull it all the way through the reed at the dent you marked with yarn. The photo shows the second end being sleyed, and you can see the already sleyed first end. Its extra length, lying over the shuttle race until you get each inch slip knotted, will make the warps less likely to slide out of the reed.

Slip knot the half inch of warps—in this case four—in front of the reed. Keeping the beater at a slight angle toward you during this step will prevent it flopping back and forth as you continue the sleying. The weight of the beater and reed combined will tend to keep the beater steady against the slip knotted ends.

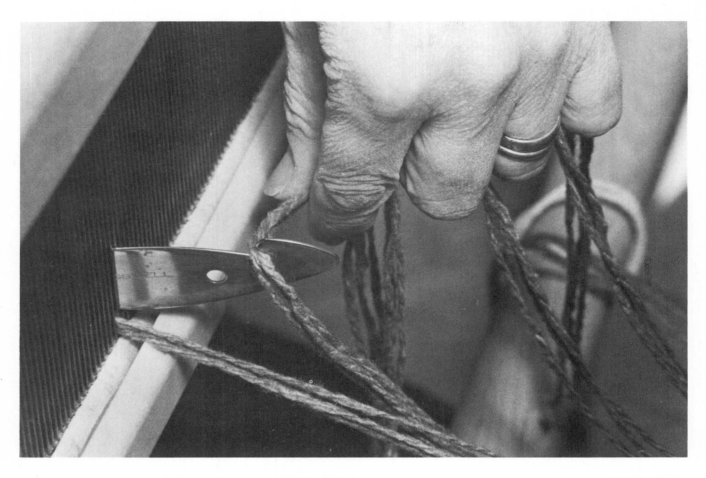

slightly acute angle toward you, the reed will not flop back and forth as you continue to sley.

The next group to be slip knotted will consist of eight ends. Inch bundles are tied on at the front, with the exception of the selvedges that are tied on in half inches.

Should you only have an 8D reed and wish to sley at 24 epi, each dent will have three ends in it; therefore, when you pick the ends with your left hand, there will be triple ends between each pair of your fingers.

In the picking process be careful to make sure you are getting the ends in correct order from the heddles as they were threaded. If you do not you will get crossed threads; and if you get crossed threads you will not get a proper shed; and if you do not get a proper shed you will not have a perfect pattern; and you probably will have broken warps as well.

Correcting Crossed Threads

Now seems a good time to say that crossed threads will show up in the first pick or two of the weaving and are very easy to fix.

You find the two offending ends—untie at the front, remove carefully from the reed, and replace in the correct order.

Should you have a really serious sleying error—for instance, a couple of inches of four ends in a dent instead of three—you will have to correct to the nearest selvedge. That is, pull out all the ends from, and including, the error to the selvedge.

Perhaps it will cheer you on to say that sleying, even careful sleying, is a simple and quick procedure.

Check the Warp Width After Sleying

When you have all the ends sleyed and slip knotted by inches as you go, you can sit back and again reach for the tape or ruler. Check to be sure the warp still measures what your notes say it should. This is not as overly cautious as it would seem. If you usually do three to a dent, and the telephone rings and it is snowing and your milkman has not shown up, you can make a mistake. I know and it wasn't even snowing.

Do not suddenly decide because it is 12" (30.5 cm) wide due to incorrect sleying, you will weave it off at 12" (30.5 cm). Since that warp was wound on at a 14" (36 cm) width, it should be woven off at the same width. Remember, you are striving for a straight feed from back to front including all steps.

You can, and you certainly may if you have a warp that will take the harsh treatment, tie on at the 12" (30.5 cm) width, wind the whole warp forward, and then rewind it at the 12" (30.5 cm) width after changing the inches of warp on the dowels. I have seen it done successfully, but I still feel re-sleying is more time saving. If after correctly sleying you suddenly feel you want a 12" (30.5 cm) not a 14" (36 cm) warp, take an inch out from the reed and heddles at either selvedge, pull them back, slip knot, and let them lie just forward of the back beam where they won't bother anyone including you. You might use them later on as cord trim for this project, or as a twisted belt.

While on the subject of reeds, here is another not-so-casual note to put into your memory box. If you ever attend a sale of secondhand weaving equipment and see a rusty reed in a size you yearn for, buy it. Also buy some ordinary household oil and very fine steel wool. A

To sley at 24 epi using an 8D reed, take three ends between each pair of fingers, because the four spaces times three equals twelve, and the four spaces are a half inch.

If you don't take the threads in order, you will get crossed threads, and that will cause all sorts of problems—easily solvable but avoidable. You can see the crossed threads are preventing a clean shed, which you need for inserting the weft.

few hours of careful rubbing will reward you with a shining oily reed. Wipe it off with a cloth, but do not wash it off with ammonia (which would obviously be the sensible thing to do). That reed is *not* stainless steel, and you want the faintest hint of protective oil on it always. Also you should first use it for a project that must be washed before use—wall hangings no, aprons yes.

Sleying in a "Wrong" Size Reed

Sleying is a procedure in which you rapidly improve. Soon you will be saying to yourself—all right, I have an 8D reed, want a sett of 6 epi, no problem, XXXO, XXXO. The X's are the dents with an end in, and the O's are dents with no end in. Because you understand that the reed determines the density of the cloth, you can accept that if you have sleyed at 6 epi, even though in an 8D reed, 6 epi is what you will get.

Yes, there will be reed marks in the cloth. And no, they will not always wash out. But the 8D reed is what you have, so what good will worrying accomplish? If you have made, washed, and pressed your sample, you know what to expect.

Just get on with the project, and remember to enjoy the doing as well as the result.

Skipping Dents On Purpose

If you are ridiculously low on warp but not on weft, and want the latter to show a good deal, you could skip a certain number of dents regularly across the warp as you sley. There it will show the weft uncrossed by warp, of course. Should you decide on this adventure, be very sure your warps or wefts—preferably both—are very fuzzy so they will stick to each other. This way the warp will not slide into the unsleyed areas where you have weft only. Wall hangings and curtains are projects that come to mind here.

If you have a half inch sleyed at 20 epi (in other words 10 sleyed in a half inch) and you skip a half inch of the reed, the warp will have been *made* at 10 epi and put on the raddle at 10 epi.

I thought I would bring this up because some beginners don't think of mechanics while they think of design possibilities—and that goes for the rest of us too, more often than it should.

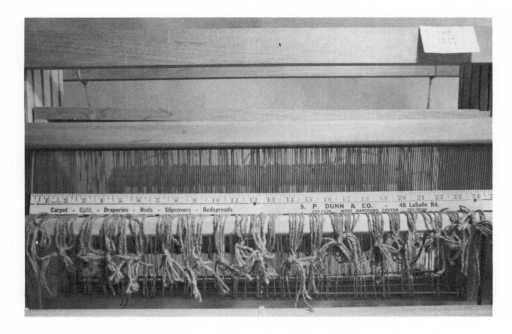

Before you tie on at the front, do measure to be sure your warp is the wanted 24" (61 cm)—or whatever—width you decided upon. The extra seconds spent are for insurance and in weaving, as in life, having insurance is wise.

6.
Tying-On

Tying-on is the term for attaching the warp—which has been wound around the warp beam and then threaded and sleyed—to the front roller.

As with many weaving procedures, there is no right or wrong way to do this; however, you should try the various methods in use to find the one that's best for you.

What You Are Trying to Achieve
The first point is to understand what you are trying to do. Regardless of the approach, the goal is to have all those bundles of warp yarns, straight across the whole warp, tied on at an absolutely even tension. If this is achieved, the weaving will come along as a straight line at 90° to the warp. If this is *not* achieved, there will be dips and arcs in the weft line, and the cloth will never be uniform in looks or density.

Fortunately, various methods have been worked out through the ages, so reaching this goal is no real problem.

How to Achieve It
One method, very good for items like scarves and stoles where you want fringe on them, is to actually tie on the warp.

Look at the front (cloth) roller and you will see a bar. Perhaps it is inside the hem of the front apron. If no front apron exists, cords nailed to the front roller may be there instead. By some method, a bar is attached to the front roller.

If you have the cords and bar assembly, loosen the bar with whatever gear and ratchet system you have. Loosen it enough so that the bar may be brought up and then over the front beam, thus lying in the actual weaving space that is between the front beam and the beater.

Now take up the middle inch of your warp ends. Untie the slip knot, so that you have an inch of warp ends loose in your hands. Divide them in half and take each half down over the bar and up again from the back. Pull to get an even tension and tie the first knot, the overhand (which you use to tie your shoes).

Pick up the next inch, either to the left or right of center, and repeat the process. Strive for the same tension. Keep alternating, left for an inch or two and then right for an inch or two, until you get to the selvedge half inch. Do the selvedge half inch as well.

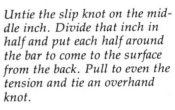

Untie the slip knot on the middle inch. Divide that inch in half and put each half around the bar to come to the surface from the back. Pull to even the tension and tie an overhand knot.

Do the same with the next inch and zigzag across the warp. Do a few inches to the left, then do a few inches to the right. Before you finish, the center inches will be loose, as you can see from the photo. Go back and tighten those overhand knots, first pulling them toward the beater. If you decide on this as your tying on method, learn to love retying because you will probably have to do it three—or more—times per warp.

By now, even on a quite narrow warp, the center inches will be quite loose. Go back and do the same thing over again, but this time you will only have to take up the ends and tighten them after pulling toward the beater. Sometimes this has to be done two or three times to insure even tension across the warp.

The last step is to give a final pull on each bundle, starting from center, and tie the rest of the bow knot sequence for each bundle. Run your hands lightly over the warp to make sure it is at an even tension. You might say this is your last chance to get it right. Actually you can perfectly well undo a bow knot and redo it after a few picks of starter weft—*not* the real weft—have been put in.

Tighten your tension further by whatever means your particular loom has. Use the front system if the bow knots are so close to the beater you can see there will be no room to put a shuttle of weft through a shed. Use the back system if you can see there is too much room in the front, and the beater will have to practically hit the front beam before it places the weft.

The old weavers' rule was "as tight a warp as can be made without injuring the warp." If you break warp threads, obviously it is too tightly stretched.

Should you have a loom apron with the bar in the hem of the apron, this method can be used with the addition of another bar tied to the first one using three fine nylon cord loops snitched through the slits that are sure to be in the hem.

With a Brand New Loom. One exception may exist. You may have a brand new loom and the loom maker made no slits in the apron—he left that so you could put them where you want them. I would recommend making three slits parallel to the selvedges, approximately an inch or two in from each side, and one at the center. Cut them short and use pinking shears if possible, so that they will stay neat looking longer.

This method of tying on a warp is very traditional, most acceptable in many workshops, beloved by some weavers, and it does work. In my opinion, more cannot be said for it.

Another Method

Now to another method of tying on. Let us mentally go back to the stage when those warp threads had all been sleyed and laid in inch bunches, slip knotted of course, in front of the beater.

Starting at one selvedge, un-slip knot each inch, give a tug to insure even tension on each thread of the bundle, and re-slip knot as close to the end as you can do it. Try to do this very close to the ends, but be sure all warp ends are caught in the knot.

When you have done this right across the warp, cut and burn a long—perhaps three or four times the warp width—piece of nylon cord.

Interruption—Nylon Burns Like Sugar! A slight interruption seems necessary here, after re-reading that cut and burn phrase. Nylon is spun from a sort of syrup I am told; but no matter what its origins, nylon has no tooth or fuzz like natural fibers. It is slick and smooth. When you cut it, the raveling starts immediately. It is easy to prevent this, but requires caution. Have ready a cup of water and a lit candle. After you have cut the nylon cord, put a cut end into the candle flame for a few seconds. You will see a blob, like burned sugar, form. Believe me it burns like scorched sugar. To prevent the burning of fingers or a hand, stick the hot blobby end of the cord into the water for a few seconds. This may seem like a lot of words for a minor point, but if you burn yourself on melted nylon, I don't want it on my conscience when common caution could have prevented it.

You have your cut and burned cord, your knotted bundles of warp, and a bar on the front roller to which you are able to attach the warp. That bar is either the one you just attached with the three loops snitching it to the apron, or it is the one attached directly to the cloth beam with cords.

Give a final gentle tug on the center inch, and finish off by tying a bowknot. Tie your bowknots across alternately on each side of the center out to the selvedges.

Run your fingers lightly across the warp to be sure the tension is as even as you can get it. Maybe you will have to redo an inch, but you probably will be fortunate and not have to.

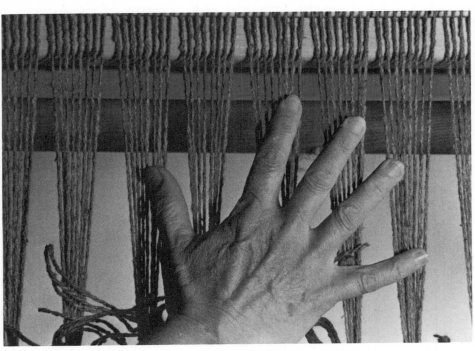

The easiest method of getting the warp evenly attached to the front roller seems to be by lashing it to the bar with the cord.

First, tie the cord to the bar and take it down on through the middle of the selvedge bundle of warp threads. Do this *above* the knot (*toward the beater*) then up over the bar and so on across the warp, finishing with a firm knot on the bar.

Because you have used a slick nylon cord, it will slide well over the bar and will not hang up in the warp bundles, no matter what the warp material (even mohair). Let us now take advantage of that quality to even up the tension.

Another approach, and one that will save you warp length, is to reslip knot straight across the warp. While doing this, try to get the knots close to ends of the warps and the tension even.

Tie the slip knotted inches to the front bar with the cut and burned nylon cord. Knot the cord to the bar. Take the other end down through a slip knotted inch above the knot and toward the beater, and then back up over the bar to the next inch, finishing with a knot on the bar.

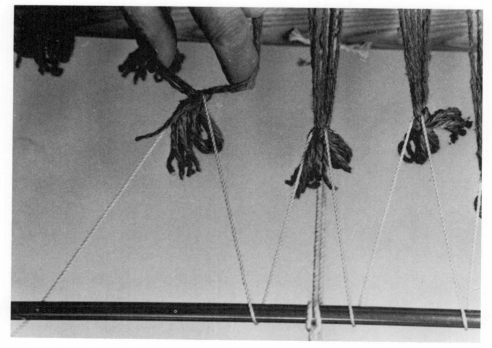

Evening Tension

Slightly tighten your warp with the front or the back crank/lever/wheel as in the previous tying on method, and again run your hand lightly over the warp. If you have a loose bundle, start plucking the cord V-shapes on either side of the loose bundle. Do the same thing if you have a tight bundle. Somehow or other the warp is becoming more even; if you continue the plucking action right across the warp a couple of times, you will find it becomes very even.

There, now you have tied on a warp. We may have removed the mystique from the procedure, but the job is acceptably done—and that was the original goal.

Left
Let's even the warp tension by the front or back crank/lever/ or whatever. Use the front assembly if the warp bundles are much too close to the beater for weaving to be done.

Top Right
Use the back system if the knots are so close to the breast beam that the beater would hit it while you are weaving.

Bottom Right
When the warp is tensioned and in a reasonable position, start plucking the cord V's on either side of any loose bundles. Do the same either side of any tight bundles. Things are getting better! Perhaps tighten the front ratchet a notch, and pluck right across the warp again. The slick nylon cord, a small matter of physics and—in my opinion—a touch of magic combine to give you a fine even warp.

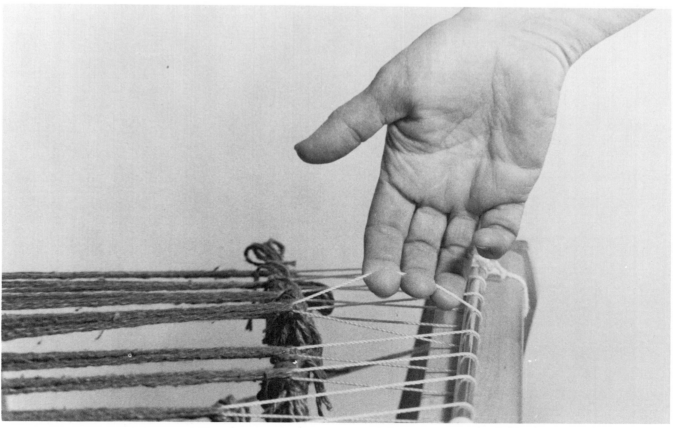

7.
Reading a Pattern

Reading a pattern is one of those nice, handy little tricks that makes you feel more self-confident; therefore, I recommend it as a skill to have like making good hollandaise sauce or raising delphinium from seed. Another thing, it is easy.

A Good Thing to Know . . .
The learned lesson can be applied to a number of uses; anyway, I think they are far beyond anything that immediately occurs to the new weaver.

The other day I made myself a woven watchband because mine had broken and my leatherworking husband was away on a trip. I took a part of a very involved coverlet pattern, centered it on the .8″ (.20 cm) wide warp at 60 epi, and was very pleased with the result. It also proved to my Saturday weaving class of teenagers that relatively fashionable items can be made from two-hundred-year-old designs, which was the prime reason for taking the time to weave the watchband.

Many people say they don't want to take the time to learn pattern reading because they only want to do wall hangings.

Often my answer is that two of the most effective wall hangings I ever saw were done by near beginners who had mastered the technique of pattern reading.

One wall hanging was on a white rosepath threaded warp. The wefts were bands of reds, roses, fuchsias, and purples. Each band—in differing widths—was done with its own treadling sequence, separated from the next color by bands of white weft, woven tabby. Most effective on a fireplace wall of white painted brick, with dark blue couches in the foreground.

The other hanging was technically unwise but extremely effective. In the first place, the color combination was great for the room—mustard warp and a very dark rust weft. The design was one huge blooming leaf motif that was carefully extracted from a coverlet threading.

The pattern weft was of too high a twist to give the look of the solid blocks of old blue and white coverlets; the lack of loft in that rust yarn tended to keep each strand separate. But it was splashily joyful, very well woven, and the colors carried it through successfully.

The Four Elements to a Draft
The elements of a pattern are really four no matter what language I have seen them written in, and no matter how simple or complex. I will call these elements A, B, C, and D, and move them about in various ways.

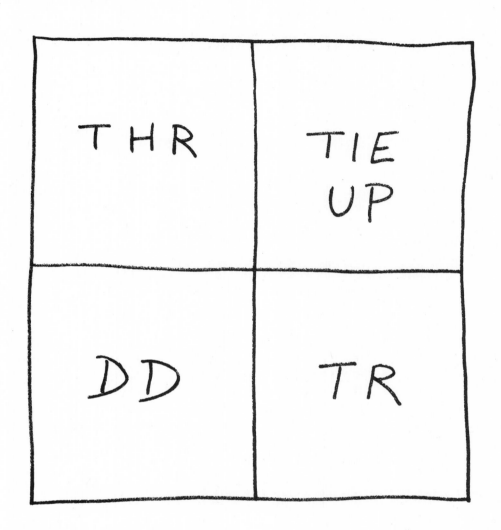

A complete draft is composed of four elements.

Clockwise
A. Threading (THR): *directions for the order in which the ends are to be put through heddles on the various harnesses.*

B. Tie-Up: *directions for what harnesses are to be tied to which treadles.*

C. Treadling (TR): *directions for the order in which you will depress the treadles.*

D. Drawdown (DD): *the weave pattern that will result. This is not necessarily the apparent pattern.*

The First Element Is Threading (A). If we think of the four elements as quarters of a vertical graph paper rectangle, the upper left quarter could be element A—the threading. This is the order of the threads going through the heddles. Should you be right-handed, you will read (and thread the heddles) from the right.

With the threading pattern 1 4 1 2 3 2, the most right-hand thread on the lease sticks will go through the most right-hand heddle on harness 2. This harness is the second closest to you as you sit at the loom. The next most right-hand thread on the lease sticks will go through the most right-hand heddle on harness 3. And this harness is behind the one you just used, and next to the back harness if you are sitting in front of a four-harness loom.

Whatever your pattern to be threaded across the warp, you will mentally pick up the pattern and lay it down again and again across the warp, as if cutting out and laying down a row of identical cookies.

Should you be left-handed, read (and thread the heddles) from the left; be sure to start with a heddle to the left side of the loom.

With a pattern of 14 threads, 1 2 3 4 3 4 3 4 1 2 1 2 3 4, I find it easier to make up a special threading sheet, which breaks the pattern into units of four (because we pick up four threads at a time). The threading sheet is an insignificant little card or square of paper securely taped to the loom in a position that is easy to read. It will look like this on the threading sheet if you are right-handed:

1234
3412
3434
12

Left-handers thread just as they (or right-handers) read, but right-handers must remember to read from right-to-left on each line. Here is a left-handed threading sheet:

1234
3434
1212
34

That way, if the telephone rings, I can stick a pin in the paper at the number of the end I have just finished, and know where I am when I come back. Should the pattern be more complicated, I still try to keep my sheet as simple as possible.

3 4 3 4 3 4 3 4 3 4 3 4 3 4 would become 34 8× (1 2 3 4) and, if I have picked up my four ends and threaded them 34 twice and am interrupted, the pin goes in at one. This indicates to me I have finished one unit of the four, each being of four ends.

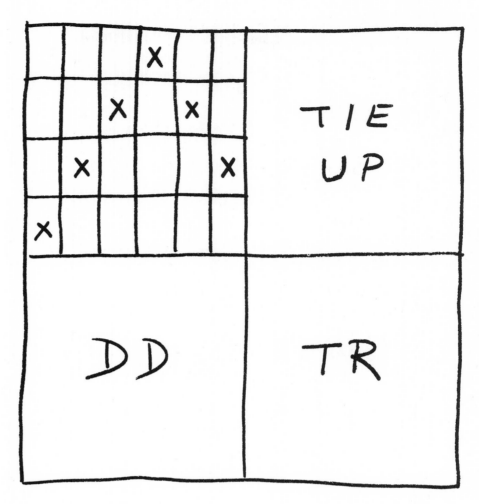

In this case the threading pattern is
1 2 3 4 3 2, 1 2 3 4 3 2, and you are
being told to repeat this six thread
unit of threading right across your
warp.

If you are right handed, you will
start threading at the right side of the
loom. For each *threading unit* you
will start with an end on harness 2,
and finish with an end on harness 1.

If you are left handed, you will
start threading at the left side of the
loom. For each *threading unit* you
will start with an end on harness 1
and finish with an end on harness 2.

Right handers thread from the
right—on both loom and pattern. Left
handers thread from the left—on both
loom and pattern.

The Second Element Is the Tie-Up (B). Element B, or the upper right-hand quarter of the graph paper, is the tie-up. This is the method by which the treadles are tied to the harnesses. It is still called the tie-up even if it is a table loom that has only levers to be pulled down or pushed up. It is also still called a tie-up when it is a four-harness direct tie-up floor loom that has four treadles instead of the usual six. Incidentally, on that loom you never re-tie, not until the cords wear out.

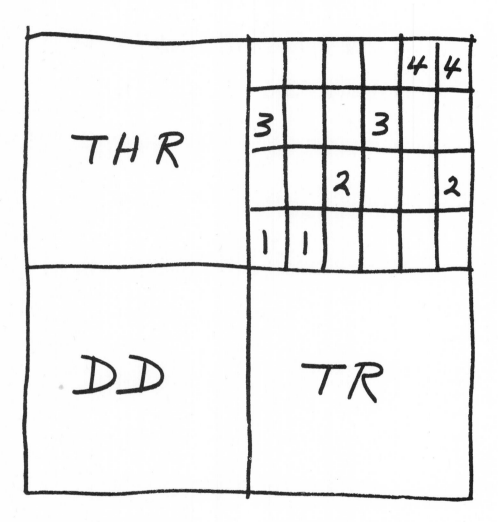

Here are directions for one way of tying up a six treadle loom.

No. 1 treadle is tied up to be Tabby A = activating harnesses 1 and 3, written 13.

No. 2 treadle activates only harness 1.

No. 3 treadle activates only harness 2.

No. 4 treadle activates only harness 3.

No. 5 treadle activates only harness 4.

No. 6 treadle is tied up to be Tabby B = activating harnesses 2 and 4, written 24.

When you depress treadle 1 on a rising shed loom, harnesses 1 and 3 will rise, thus making every end threaded on those harnesses rise.

When you depress treadle 1 on a sinking shed loom, harnesses 1 and 3 will sink, thus making every end threaded on those harnesses sink.

Let us assume this is a rising shed loom.

Should you want to raise all the ends on harnesses 2 and 3 and 4, put one foot on treadles 3 and 4 and the other on treadle 5; or one foot on treadle 3 and the other on treadles 4 and 5; or one foot on treadle 6 and the other on treadle 4.

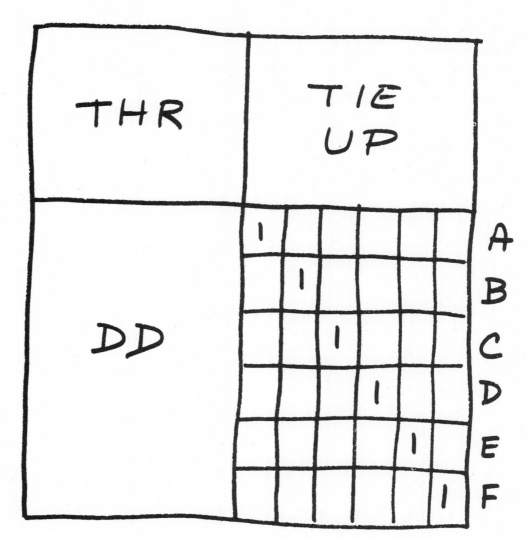

Here are treadling directions, and they are to be read by moving down, one line at a time, from A to F.

Each letter equals a pick of weaving. And you will open the shed, throw the shuttle, beat and change the shed to the one indicated by the next letter.

The Third Element Is Treadling (C). If you can imagine that Element C, which is the lower right-hand quarter of the paper, refers to your feet on the treadles (or your hands on the levers of a table loom) then you begin to see what actually happens.

Element C has some X's, some colored-in blocks, or some virgules to indicate what treadles to use when. Start with the mark that is closest to Element B of the pattern, and continue moving on down, one stroke at a time, with a card held parallel to the top of the paper.

The pattern is telling you what to do, in very clear terms, to achieve the result you have chosen. All you have to do is learn the language, and fortunately there are few irregular verbs in weaving.

The first stroke refers straight up to harnesses 1 and 2. You know that because there is an indication for harness 1 on the same line as number 1 in the threading pattern. It also refers to harness 2, and you know that because there is an indication for harness 2 on the same line as number 2 in your pattern threading.

The treadling direction wants you to activate harnesses 1 and 2 simultaneously, and put your shuttle of weft through the resulting open space, called a shed.

If you have a floor loom with six treadles, this could be done by tying harnesses 1 and 2 to the first treadle, and then depressing that treadle.

If you have a floor loom with four treadles only, depress the left-hand two treadles.

If you have a table loom, activate the first two levers.

In any of the three cases (if you have a warp tied onto the loom) you will then have a shed through which a pick, shot (or row, if you started your craft life as a knitter) of weft can be put.

The Fourth Element Is the Drawdown (Or Drawup) (D). Now we come to the lower left-hand quarter of the paper. This is known as the drawdown—or drawup (take your choice). It is the area where the pattern you propose to weave will show on your graph paper.

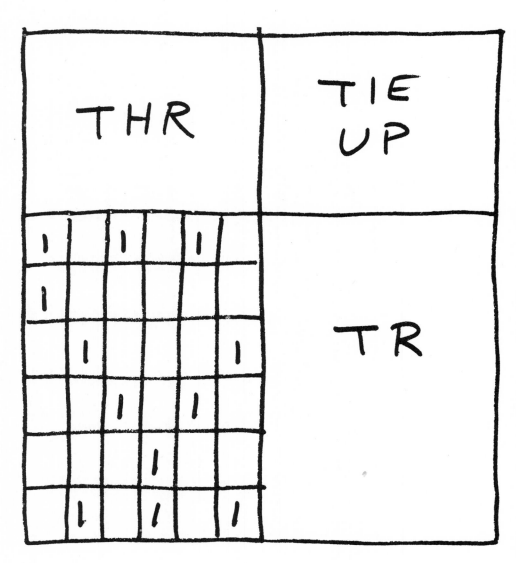

When you have threaded as in the THR (threading) diagram, tied your treadles as in the TIE-UP diagram, treadled as in the TR (treadling) diagram, you will get the weave pattern as in the DD (drawdown) section.

Again we shall assume that this loom is a rising shed model.

Line B in the TR section (page 59) says to raise harness 1. When that is done all the ends on that harness are raised.

All the warp ends on harness 1 will be over the wefts, as those ends on that harness were raised out of the way and the weft went under them. The warp will be under all the ends on harnesses 2, 3, and 4 because they were left alone, so the weft went over them.

That is the reason for the vertical lines in every DD box relating to harness 1, to give you a picture of the warp ends on harness 1 lying over the weft for that pick.

If you cut a cardboard L and use it to fill in your drawdown section, you will find the job noticeably easier.

Do that first in pencil, and then when you are convinced you have done it right, go over the job in ink or—better yet—the color(s) of the warp.

Translating from Paper to Loom

It is a sort of an eggnog, or a garden: Eggs, plus sugar, plus milk, plus salt, plus vanilla, equals eggnog; seeds, plus earth, plus water, plus fertilizer, plus sun, equals a garden.

What they are telling you is that, having threaded the loom to a certain pattern A, tied the treadles as they direct you at B, and using the treadles in the order indicated at C, you will get the pattern at D.

Reading the Same Design at 40 epi or 10 epi. You will get that pattern in miniature if you have threaded it at 40 ends per inch, and you will get it much larger if you have threaded it at 10 ends per inch, four times as large to be exact. But the pattern will never vary. If it is to be a diamond—it will be a big, small, red, blue, shiny, dull, bright or subtle diamond. But a diamond it will remain. As they say in the ads, diamonds are forever.

Rising Shed or Sinking, Book and Loom

It is wise to know what sort of a pattern book you are dealing with— a rising shed (the loom structure pulls the harnesses up) or a sinking shed (vice versa) book. Most of the modern books and looms are rising shed, and this is usually stated somewhere at the beginning of the book. But the most used pattern book I know, *A Handweaver's Pattern Book* by Marguerite Davison, is a sinking shed book.

Here is a fairly standard graph direction for tying up a loom. This one happens to be for a rising shed loom.

To change so the same pattern will appear on the top surface on a sinking shed loom, "tie up the blanks" as some weaving books say.

For example, column A has harnesses 1 and 3 tied up now. To "tie-up the blanks" you would untie 1 and 3 and tie 2 and 4.

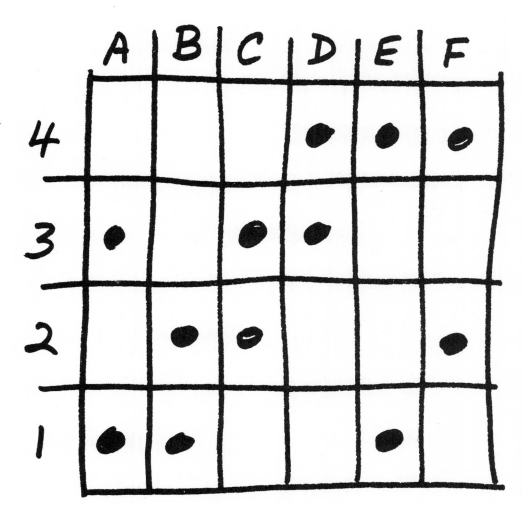

If you use her book on a rising shed loom, the pattern will come out on the wrong side—unless you change the tie-up to all opposites, or tie up the blanks, as many books say. You take the tie-up column for a pattern and find that each vertical division has some X'd boxes and some blank boxes. Tie the blank boxes, not the X'd boxes.

If you use two colors you like, say a bright warp and a single, subtly contrasting color weft, this whole thing becomes not only very clear but often quite lovely. Also it is usually better on one side than the other.

Suppose you have a red warp mostly hidden by gray weft on one side for one pick. Remember the opposite is going to happen on the other side; this means you will have a gray weft mostly hidden by the red warp as reverse.

How to Change One Method to the Other. It is nice to be able to reverse a pattern, so you can see which side you prefer; and it is embarrassingly easy.

Suppose your pattern is in the treadling at A below. Do that for 2" or so of the sample. Then do the complete opposite treadling for the same distance.

A	*Reverse of A*
1	234
234	1
13	24
124	3
4	123
23	14

You now have, facing upward, first the right and then the wrong sides of your pattern. Looking at the underside of the weaving with a purse mirror, you can see in the same order first the wrong side and then the right side of your pattern.

If you prefer the "wrong" pattern and have a lot of yards to weave, wouldn't you rather look at *it* for the yards of weaving, than the side you will not be using? So there is another advantage to this simple trick.

A Drawdown Is Really a Drawup

The elements of this pattern reading sheet can be rearranged to a certain extent. For example:

A—Threading	B—Tie-up
D—Drawdown	C—Treadling

can change to:

D—Drawdown	C—Treadling
A—Threading	B—Tie-up

In the second situation, the drawdown quarter will really be a draw*up*, though it is still referred to as a drawdown. Its advantage here is that it really appears as you would weave it, while the true drawdown does not. When you weave, you weave up. Pick one, and pick two, and then pick three. If the first three picks are the top of a Christmas tree, it looks great on a drawdown. On a drawup, or an actual weaving, it might not appeal to your sense of humor.

Here is another example of the true drawdown. Suppose your weaving pattern showed a woven doll. If you followed those treadling directions exactly, your resulting doll would be standing on her head. This may look like an unimportant carp, but you might want to put in some design for which you have the treadling directions. You would do well to draw it—either up or down—to see which way it will turn out, as you wish it or upside down.

Or to Put It Another Way

To make a drawdown—or a drawup—you must understand the functions of each of the four quarters that made up the vertical rectangle on graph paper.

We could sum up by saying A is the threading. The representation of actual warp threads, and how they go through the heddles—in other words, to what harness each end is assigned.

B is the tie-up. How the cords, chains or pins are attached (usually indirectly) from the harnesses to the individual treadles.

C is the treadling pattern. How it is indicated is irrelevant. Some mark on each line below the tie-up will refer right back up to the tie-up. This mark tells you to do something with a particular treadle. And the only reasonable thing to do with a treadle is to press it with your foot. When you do that you will get a certain pattern of threads rising and one of threads staying where they are, though they appear to be falling. If you change to the next treadle, granted it is tied to another combination of harnesses, you will get another pattern of threads rising and threads apparently falling. And this is one way patterns are formed.

Your job now is to translate the treadling directions onto the lower left-hand section, Element D, so the pattern appears there as it will on the actual woven piece.

Supposing your mythical warp is threaded 1 2 3 4 3 2 right across itself. There are only two treadles tied up. One is tied to 13 and the other is tied to 24. This is a rising shed loom, the sheds being formed by certain harnesses rising. (Not so surprisingly, a sinking shed loom operates by certain harnesses sinking and thus forming a shed.)

Therefore, when the first horizontal mark is directly below the 13, it means that straight across the warp *all* heddles (and the ends in them) in harnesses 1 and 3 will rise. If your warp is green and weft is red (heaven forfend) all the ends on harnesses 1 and 3 will cover the weft you will place for that shot. Now go straight across your little graph paper, using a ruler or card edge, marking a vertical pencil dash directly under each 1 and 3 of the threading. It is a vertical mark because you are raising those warp ends and—in effect—putting a weft under each one.

The next treadle indicated for you to use is obviously the other one. Slide your ruler down one horizontal and, referring back up to the threading, put a vertical pencil dash on the new row, just below the previously marked 13 row, but only at each and every 2 and 4.

Do this a couple of times and then sit back and relax. Now look at your diagram. You have a tiny checkerboard, because every other end, on one pick, shows. On the next pick, the alternate ends show. And the same is true for the weft covered ends. Or you could say the odd ends show in one pick, and the evens in the next one.

The oldest, simplest weaving pattern in the world is plain weave, tabby, 1/1, one up and one down, tapestry—call it what you will. Use it for cloth weaving, paper weaving, baskets, leather, it is still plain weave.

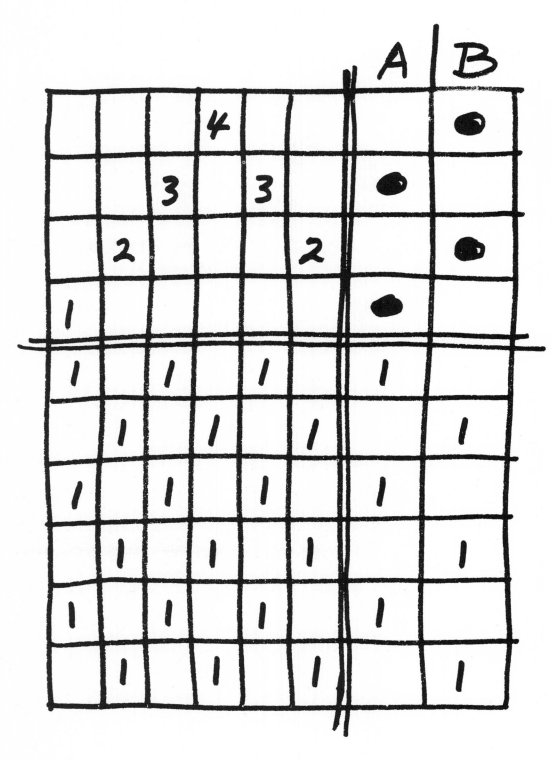

You have a threading pattern of 1 2 3 4 3 2, only two treadles tied up, and are to treadle A and then B and repeat.

With warp of one color and weft of another, you will get a checkerboard in the drawdown section.

Making Your Own Simple Drawdown

Let's start all over. 1 2 3 4 3 2 is still the threading. Put that in position A. This time, let's use four treadles. Tie up as follows:

No. 1 to 12
No. 2 to 23
No. 3 to 34
No. 4 to 14

All that will be marked in your section B. For the treadling, let us do a horizontal V, and do it 1 2 3 4 3 2. That means put a mark at treadle 1, then at treadle 2, one row below it, and so on.

When your ruler goes under the first treadling direction, you will see that instead of every other thread being raised and the opposite one lowered, here is a whole new situation. As you progress, it gets more interesting.

Sometimes you have three consecutive ends raised or not raised. Sometimes there is one raised or not raised. On some picks that red weft only peeks out above one warp end, then dives under for two or three ends. If you will repeat the treadling sequence again, that is, 1 2 3 4 3 2—you will see a distinct pattern emerge.

This is the pattern you will get with a warp of one color, a weft of another, and the threading, tie-up and treadling as above.

One unit of the treadling is at the right above line B.

One unit of the resulting pattern is at the left above line B.

Here is another time when you must do more than one unit or repeat of a treadling pattern to get a good picture of the weave as it will appear when the job is finished.

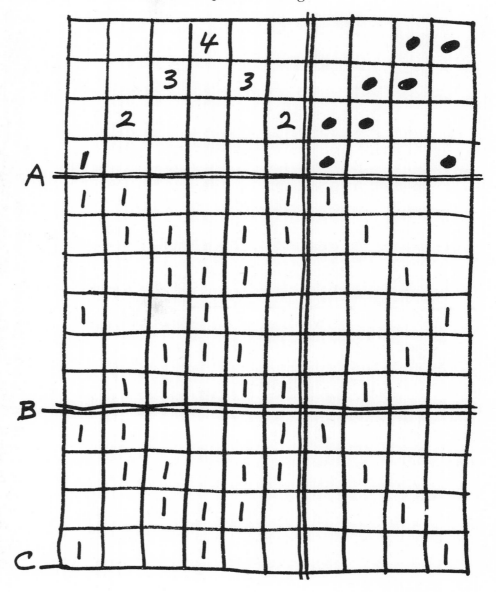

More Complex Drawdowns. Still with the horrendous red and green combination in mind, imagine what would happen if all the ends on harness four were *red* not green. How would that change your pattern? Or all those on harness 2, or even on harnesses 1 *and* 2? Try that on your graph paper. Or what happens when you use a green weft on every pick that requires the fourth treadle?

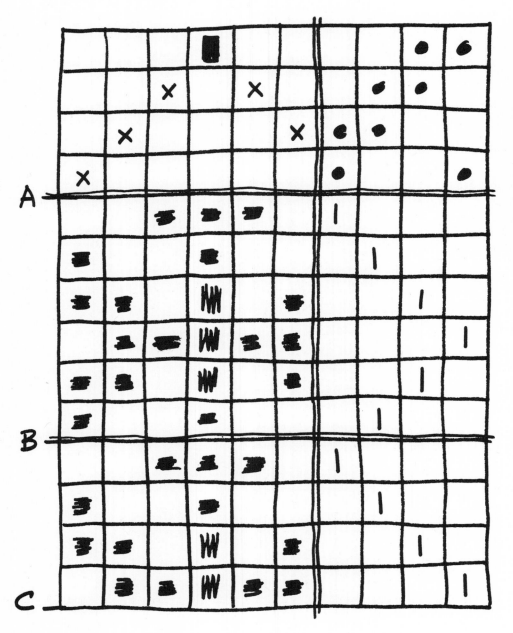

In the threading section, the black squares indicate that on harness 4 we have red ends and not green as in the rest of the warp.

Note how that changes the apparent pattern. It does not change the weave of course, but it certainly changes the appearance.

In the drawdown section all the places where the red weft shows (and also *where that red end on harness 4 shows*) have been blacked in to show the apparent pattern.

This is but another way of noting different colors in the warp and weft.

In the drawdown section only the places where the warp shows have been indicated so far.

To show how the finished weaving would appear, fill in the blank squares in the drawdown section with the two different letters indicated in the treadling directions—R is for the first 3 picks, G for the next 3, and R for the last one in the complete treadling unit.

If you do the whole job first with pencil and then with two colors of marking pen or pencil, the picture is really clear.

Symbols for Color Changes

Using a symbol to indicate a different color—in either warp or weft—will preserve your reason. With no colored pencils at hand, I use X's for the first color in a warp, the next is a circle, the next a square, the next could be a vertical dash or a triangle, and so on. The same code can go for the weft directions in the treadling, *if the colors are the same as the warp colors.*

Absolutely the easiest way I know to indicate color change in the weft, when you are using only two colors there, is to circle the treadle number with the second color, when you are writing the treadling sheet to be pinned or taped to the loom. Most of the time I use only two colors in the weft, so that may well be why it is so simple for me. Doubtless there are other methods as labor saving. Different colored pens, underlining—whatever seems simplest for you.

Berta Frey once said to do the drawdowns lightly in pencil, and *then* go over them with the various colored marking pens. This is good advice because you will soon discover marking pen is a bit harder to erase than pencil.

It is not usual to put in the horizontal weft color strokes, the draw-down where the warp has *not* risen; but if you want to, it certainly shows the color play better.

If you are wondering why I used red and green, admittedly a terrible color combination, the explanation is simple. If you *do* it—even on graph paper alone—you will see it is such an appalling color idea that you will never try it out for Christmas items or for anything else. And that is what I was trying to prevent.

8.
Making a Warp

If you think this chapter is going to be a repetition of Chapter 1, it isn't. You will have to go back to it for directions on tying crosses, choke ties, warp winding, etc.

This chapter will try to apprise you of some of the very different problems that will arise with longer, wider warps.

How to Make a 36″ (91 cm) Wide Warp on a Frame
Let us start out with a common wider warp problem. Suppose you have a 36″ (91 cm) loom and wish to put on a 36″ (91 cm) wide warp, but have only a warping frame on which to make it. You will probably find it easier to make three individual 12″ (30.5 cm) warps, and to "put them together" on the lease sticks, and from then on to treat them like a single unit.

When you are tying the cross each time on one of the 12″ (30.5 cm) warps, be certain you do not tie the length string into it (or into a choke tie).

The length string, you will recall, was the piece of non-stretchy yarn with which you measured the desired length of the warp, plus two slip knots—one to go over the front warp peg and one to go over the back warp peg. It is always better to have the length string in a color that sharply contrasts with the warp color because it is easier to avoid tying it into the choke ties or the cross.

Mixed Fibers Warp Sample
Eventually you will mix colors, textures, and weights of yarns in your warps. With disparate yarns, try very hard to plan stripes of the more stretchy yarn to be narrow, so that if the stretch factors are grossly different, you won't have as much trouble. But you may well have trouble anyway. The important thing is to make samples first. Then, if it works out successfully, go from the 3″ (8 cm) sample to the 6″ (15 cm) sample and, if that also works out, go to a wider and longer one. I am trying to prevent you going from a 3″ (8 cm) wide 30″ (76 cm) sample to a 36″ (91 cm) wide 10 yard (9.1 m) warp, and getting into serious difficulties.

No More Than Four Threads Without a Paddle
You can wind up to four threads at once on the frame or mill, if you use your fingers to keep them reasonably in order. I treat them as

one at the cross. It may not be correct, but for me it works. The old weavers gave four threads as the maximum and, since they have been proven right about so many things, I have never tried even five.

The four threads can be the same (wound on four different spools) or all different, or pairs, or three of one and an odd one. It doesn't matter at all.

Cones Wind Off Sitting Upright

If you are winding from four cones, you can prevent their tipping over by standing them on large nails that have been nailed to a board. Or you can be a perfectionist woodworker and drill holes into which you put dowels. In this case, go all the way through the wood and you will not have to worry about having to cut little grooves into the side of the dowel, so the air or glue can escape up the side.

To keep the cones sitting upright while you are winding a warp, they can be put over a board into which huge nails have been pounded, or dowels have been put.

Spools Wind Off Horizontally

If you are winding from spools, remember they are to be unwound from a horizontal position—theirs, not yours.

The easiest way I have found is to thread them onto the back bar of a loom and wind off from that. The end loops from one bar to the other hold the spools on, and so far I have had no problems. If I had some yarns that spin off wildly (perhaps something very wiry), I would have to be a traditionalist and use the bobbin creel. To use the bobbin creel I thread the yarn around a couple of the horizontal bars in and out, which reduces the speed of the unwinding by increasing the drag on the yarn.

The reason I do not use the creel other than for spool storage is that when winding a warp from it, you really should take off all the spools you are not using. If you don't do this, the vibration from the spools unwinding will make the other spools unwind, and you'll have a useless tangle of wasted threads on the floor—or, even worse, they'll wind into the warp.

Balls Wind Off From Bowls

If you are using balls, as in knitting or weaving yarns you bought as hanks and have wound into balls, just go into the kitchen and get some mixing bowls. Wind from the balls placed in the bowls.

In a pinch—in a craft center class—use tote bags (emptied first, please, for the sake of your sanity) or paper bags. But they do not work nearly as well as the bowls. One ball to a bowl keeps the tangling to a minimum.

Threaded onto the back bar of a loom and wound off from there, spools are in the correct position to wind off horizontally.

Left
A wiry, temperamental yarn on a spool can be made to wind off at a more dignified rate by using a bobbin creel. This piece of equipment enables you to feed the end of the recalcitrant spool in and out of a few of the horizontal rods before it goes to the frame. Because the drag is increased on the spool, it winds off slower and thus does not outpace the one coming from a cone, should you be winding these two types at the same time. You really should take the other spools off the creel before doing this because the vibration from the rotating spool is quite likely to start the others unwinding and tangling.

Below
Clamp your swift so it will spin vertically; a hank put on this will usually wind directly to the warping frame easily. If the yarn seems to be sticking to itself and not running freely, you will have to wind it into a loose ball as an extra step before making the warp.

Hanks Wind Off From Swifts or Squirrels

If you are fortunate enough to be in possession of a swift—which is one of those beautiful gadgets known by several different names that looks slightly like an umbrella stripped to its skeleton—clamp it to something so it will spin vertically. Put your skein/hank on it so that it winds directly to the warping frame without the intermediate winding-into-a-ball stage.

The squirrel is composed of an upright post attached to a firm base, with two horizontal cages attached one above the other. One cage is fixed in a permanent position, and the other is movable so you can adjust it to fit different sized hanks.

Two Yarns Wound as One

In case you want to wind two threads together and treat them as one, there are various devices on the market that you can buy if you are either rich or device-minded.

You can also use a cane seated chair. Put one cone on the seat and the other cone under the seat, feeding the end of the bottom cone through the chair and through the top cone. For some reason, one twists with the other, and you have one end ready-made as it winds onto the warping frame.

You could surely use a plastic webbed porch chair if you have no antique caned one due for refinishing. Or an ancient rush seated chair, with the end coming up through the center point. Or a box with a hole punched by an enormous sized knitting needle.

We seem to have accounted for all ways yarn will come to you: hanks, balls, cones, spools. There is only one other way—the pull skein—which is a source of annoyance to me since I recall when they started selling them, they charged more for the so-called convenience.

Better Wind a Pull Skein Into a Ball

When you are winding warps, you should rewind them into old-fashioned balls because the skeins do not always pull out at an even rate. And wind those balls loosely, loosely, loosely—always, always, always. There is no reason to take out the elasticity that you want and for which you have paid. Wind around your fingers for a few rounds, pull them out, and repeat until the skein has become a ball.

Always keep in mind your goal of an evenly wound warp, for which you are prepared to spend time, because you know it will save time in the long run.

Try to Wind the Warp Evenly

When you are winding the warp onto the loom—beaming the warp—do it as evenly as possible. This really is a long run time saver. It will reduce the chances of broken warps because loose ones as well as tight ones will break. Also the weaving will be easier and smoother.

A Horizontal Warping Mill Is Great

While we are on the subject of making a warp, I am quite aware that most people buy warping frames because they are cheaper than warping mills and more easily stored when not in use. But there is a marvelous little horizontal warping mill for sale from a supplier that can be used on a regular table, couch, piano bench, or coffee table. It, too, folds utterly flat when you are not in the warp making mood so it gives you more yarn room, which is as great an idea as the horizontal warping mill.

Left
One cone is on a chair, and the other is under the chair. The end from the cone on the floor is fed up through the chair seat, and then through the top cone. When this combination is wound onto the frame it has become one yarn, because they will have twisted around each other.

Right
Winding a pull skein into a ball before using it to make a warp is not really a waste of time, as pull skeins do not, in my experience at least, pull out at an infallibly uniform rate. When you make balls from these—or from hanks for that matter—wind the yarn around your fingers for a few rounds, pull them out, wind around them again and so on. The goal here is a soft ball, not a ball with which you can play softball. The tighter the ball, the more elasticity you have removed from the yarn. And remember, particularly in the case of wool, you paid high for that elasticity, so guard it carefully.

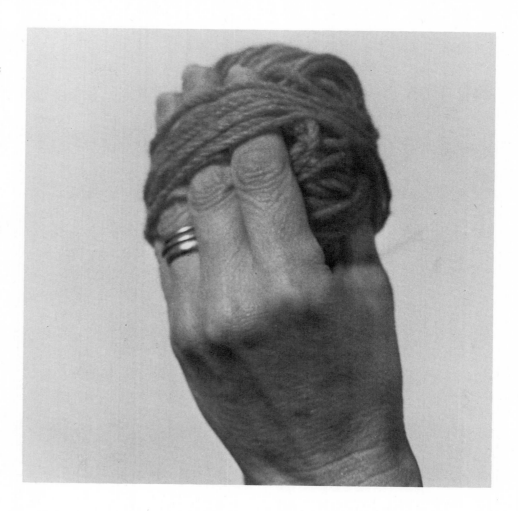

9.
Tying String Heddles

Although you probably have a loom with metal heddles—flat steel or wire—knowing how to tie string heddles is valuable. The law of probability says that some future day you will make a threading error, and this knowledge will solve that problem.

When You Will Use the Knowledge
You have just discovered a threading error, perhaps an end in harness 3 that belongs in harness 2. The first thing to do is look for the wire cutters, or old scissors if there are no wire cutters in the house. Then find a piece of string—about carpet warp strength—approximately twice the length of the heddle, plus a few inches.

Identify the wrongly threaded heddle carefully, tie a bit of bright yarn around it, and check again. I know nothing more annoying than correcting the wrong heddle—one that was fine until you monkeyed with it.

How to Make String Heddles on the Loom
Fold the string in half, snitch it over the bottom heddle bar of the *correct* harness (directly beside the wrongly threaded end), and make an overhand knot at exactly the place where the bottoms of the eyes of the other correct-harness heddles occur. A knitting needle stuck into the knot will make it slide up or down to exactly where you want it to be. Then pull the needle out. Enclose the offending end in the new string heddle, and tie an overhand knot at exactly the point where the tops of the eyes on the other heddles of that harness occur. Use the knitting needle again if you think it helps; it usually does. Now make a square knot around the top heddle bar, and cut off the long ends left from tying your string heddle.

The end is now held by heddles on two harnesses, which will not do at all.

Take the wire cutters and remove the metal heddle as neatly as you can from both the offending end and the harness. It will probably come off in pieces; gather them all neatly because they are sharp and do not mix well with bare feet or kittens.

You are now back in business.

A Jig to Make for a Loom's Worth of Them
String heddles can be tied for a whole loom, although I cannot imagine why anyone would want to. But if you need twenty more heddles

Top Left
Tie bright yarn around the wrongly threaded heddle. Check again to make sure it really is the wrongly threaded one. (You don't want to "correct" one that was correct.)

Top Right
A length of carpet warp is folded in half and shown snitched over the bottom heddle bar of the proper harness. Note that it is right beside the end you are correcting, but on the right harness. (In the photograph it is held straight up by an unseen hand, but the snitch on the heddle bar is visible.)

Bottom Left
An overhand knot has been made at the point where the bottoms of the other heddle eyes occur. On a sinking shed loom, a fraction of an inch closer to the bottom is acceptable; but on a rising shed loom the knot should be even with the lower end of the heddle eye.

Bottom Right
Make the string heddle enclose the offending end before you tie the overhand knot that completes the new heddle eye. Sinking shed looms must have this knot exactly even with the tops of the eyes of the other heddles. Rising shed looms may be a fraction of an inch off.

Tie a square knot to enclose the top heddle bar; the string heddle is now finished. Cut off some of the extra length which is probably hanging down. The wrongly threaded end is now contained by two heddles on two harnesses, which will not do at all.

for a project and have no more metal ones, or if the warp yarn is too thick to go through the metal eyes, you will have to tie string heddles.

That job requires a jig—a piece of board with four nails pounded firmly into the wood. The nails are placed so that the eyes of the heddles will be right where you want them to be. These nails must be perpendicular to the board surface in order that the tied heddles will slip off easily. Use finishing nails—no heads to get in the way.

Some Differences Between Rising and Sinking Shed Looms. Before making the jig, determine whether you have a rising shed or a sinking shed loom. If you have a rising shed loom, the shed is made by raising certain harnesses. Therefore, the *bottom* of the string heddle eye must be even with the bottom of the metal eyes. All the threads on one harness will then rise together when the heddles (metal and string) are pulled up by the action of raising the harness (and the heddle bar on which all the heddles are hanging).

With wire cutters, carefully cut away the metal heddle from the loom and the warp end. A hacksaw or old scissors will do the job if wire cutters are not in your tool inventory.

If the reverse is true and your loom is a sinking shed, the shed is made by sinking certain harnesses. Therefore the *top* of the string heddle eye must be even with the tops of the metal eyes while the pulling down action is occurring. The photo on page 80 should make that clear. Note that the bottom loop of the metal heddle hangs *below* the heddle bar. That slack, which varies with different heddles and different looms, is necessary to allow the heddles to slide onto the bars easily. The slack is taken up with the beginning of the downward movement of the harness against the tension of the warp until, a moment later, the *tops* of the metal heddle eyes apply pressure on the warp ends. That's when the tops of the string heddle eyes must come in contact with the warp.

A long explanation, but important if you want to understand the conditions necessary for a clean shed. Now let's start with serious first grade carpentry.

Jig for a Rising Shed Loom. Measure the distance from the top of the upper heddle bar to the bottom of the lower bar. This will be the length of your string heddle. It has to be that length so it will fit onto the top and bottom heddle bars without being too short or too long.

Transfer this measurement to your board and pound in two nails at the right places. With a metal heddle slipped over both nails and snugged down against the top one, pound in a nail inside the heddle eye at the *bottom* of the eye.

Now hammer in another nail about 1" (2.5 cm) above that one—and the jig is completed.

(If you have flat metal heddles with loops and eyes too small to fit over the nails, place one alongside the first two nails and carefully mark the location of the bottom of the eye before doing any hammering.)

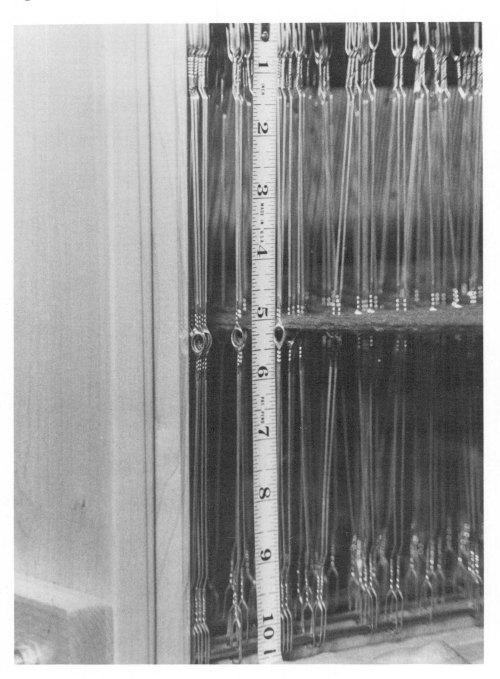

Left
To make a jig for string heddles, and the heddles themselves, for a rising shed loom, follow the steps here and on page 81. First, measure distance from top of upper heddle bar to bottom of lower bar. This will be the length of the string heddles.

Opposite Page:

Top Left
Transfer the measurement to the jig, placing nails at A and D.

Top Right
Use a metal heddle to determine the position of nail C, which must be exactly even with the bottom of the metal heddle eye when the top loop of the metal heddle is tight against nail A.

Bottom Left
Place nail B about one inch above nail C.

Bottom Right
Loop carpet warp over A; tie square knots under B, C, and D, keeping string taut but not tight. Remove heddle from jig, cut off extra string and try it on the loom. Be sure to slip the tied end under the lower heddle bar.

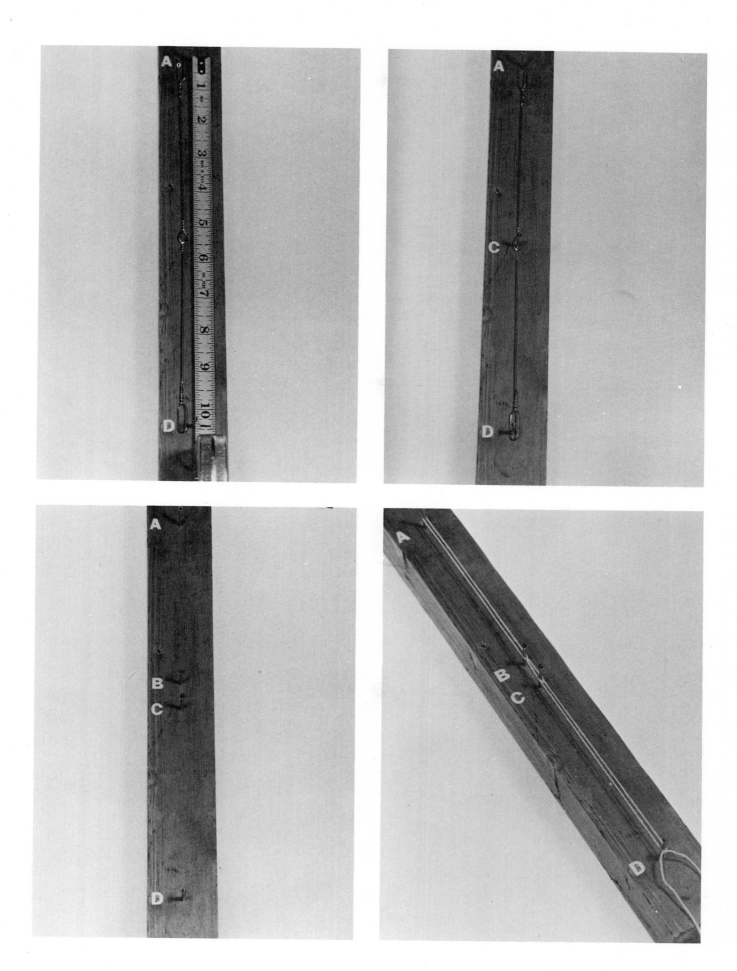

Now for the string heddles. Fold a piece of carpet warp in half and lay the curve over the top nail. Pull it taut and tie a square knot below the first nail down (this will be the top of the eye), another below the next nail (the bottom of the eye), and the last one below the bottom nail. Clip off the trailing ends and try your completed string heddle on the loom, making sure the tied end is under the lower heddle bar. If it fits, tie a dozen or more before taking them off the nails.

Jig for a Sinking Shed Loom. Again the measured distance from the top of the upper heddle bar to the bottom of the lower bar will be the length of a string heddle.

Transfer this measurement to the board, using two nails to mark the outer positions. But this time when you slip a metal heddle over the nails, push the bottom of the heddle *up* until it presses against the lower nail, leaving any slack above the upper nail.

Keep the heddle in that position while you put a nail at the *top* of the heddle eye. Then pound in another one about an inch below it. The jig is done.

To make the heddle, fold the length of carpet warp in half and lay the curve *under* the bottom nail. Pull it taut and tie a square knot *above* the next nail up, making another knot above the third nail and a final one above the top nail. Cut off the extra string and try the heddle on the loom; make sure the tied end is *over* the upper heddle bar. You can now make the quantity you need.

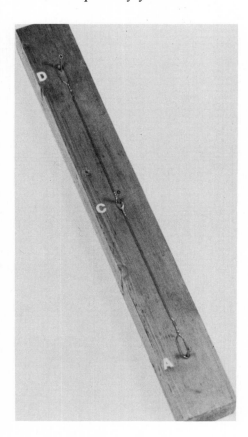
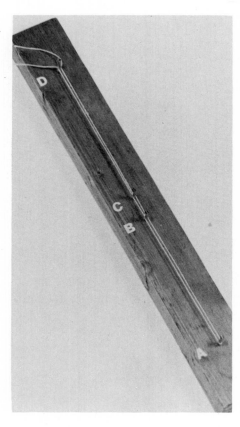

Left
For sinking shed looms that have metal heddles of the same length, use the same AD spacing as with rising shed heddles, but with nail A at the bottom of the jig and nail D at the top. To position nail C correctly, place a metal heddle on—or beside—the two nails, with the bottom loop tight against nail A. Hammer nail C into place.

Right
Place nail B about one inch below C, then loop carpet warp under A and tie square knots above B, C, and D. Remove heddle, cut off extra string and place on harness with the tied end over the top heddle bar.

10.
Leveling a Loom and Tying Treadles

In this section we shall assume you have a loom of either the jack or counter-balanced variety. Since there are so many variations of looms, I did not provide photographs of them. I felt that photographs would be confusing because you would look for features that might not be on the loom you want to level or tie. This is why I am only giving the basic principles here.

Two Types of Looms to Consider: Jack and Counter-balanced
Either type will give you a wide enough shed to throw a shuttle through only if it is properly leveled and/or tied.

The principles are a little different for the two types of looms, but they are very simple principles indeed.

Leveling a Counter-balanced Loom
Tie a length of string to the back beam, put it through any one heddle, then through the reed, and tie on to the front beam. The string should lie along the top surface of the two beams.

What You Are Seeking. When this has been done, stand at the side of the loom and look at the string. It should lie in a straight line from back beam, through heddle, through reed, and onto breast beam.

At the point where the string goes through the reed, it should lie close to the top of the reed. Remember this type of loom gets its shed by sinking harnesses, which will give you the bottom half of the shed. If the warp (and the string is a stand-in for the warp) is close to the bottom of the reed, a shed cannot be made because there is no place for the warps to sink to, since they cannot sink through the bottom of the reed.

How to Get It. If the string dips at the reed, the beater may be set too low; in this case find out where it is attached to the loom frame. You may be able to raise it by a screw adjustment; or the situation could be that the reed is too short. Short is used here as the opposite of tall—it has nothing to do with length. If the reed height is too short, it is not the reed for that particular loom because it is not high enough to do its job properly. I do not mean that it can be raised in the beater because I have never seen that possible.

Reed Differences

Reeds come not only in various lengths and various dents, but also in various heights. This is an important matter too often ignored. Forgetting this can well cause broken warps—or at best serious fraying.

How to Work Around the Wrong Reed. If the reed is too low and it is all you have available, use only strong warps. This is because all your warps will tend to wear at the top where they lie against the top member of the reed. Advance the warp more often too, minimizing the wear on a given area of the warp.

Advancing the Warp

On any loom you should only weave up to about three or four inches before you advance the warp. If the weaving area—the area where you are able to weave—is much larger than that figure, you should still weave in only the small area.

The reason is that the beater changes the angle at which it beats the weft. This could change the quality of the cloth, but it will not necessarily do so. I mention it because it is something to watch for. And with the short reed you would be wise to advance the warp before it gets chafed and frayed.

If There Is a Dip at the Heddle

If there is a dip at the heddle eye, look at the ropes above the harnesses. Some looms have an arrangement with screws and wing nuts that will raise the poles on which the harnesses are hung. If your loom has this, try it out and use your common sense as a guide. Remember you are trying to raise the heddles—and therefore the harnesses—a small fraction of an inch.

If no such built-in labor saving device exists, the ropes must be shortened to raise the harnesses. Many of the more modern counterbalanced looms have a shortening system for the ropes that is roughly the equivalent of shoulder straps on full slips or bras. But the slide for the loom is a lot tougher on fingernails, so you will want to use a short knitting needle, or something like that, as a fid to loosen the ropes.

If the loom is really old, you will have to untie knots to change the level of the rollers. Do not retie a hard and fast knot before you are quite certain you have solved the problem to your satisfaction.

Finally the string lies flat on the back beam, to the heddles, through the reed, and lies on the breast beam; all this is in a nice straight line.

Now Check the Treadles Mechanism. Look under the loom. Where the harnesses are attached to lamms (the bars to which the treadles are tied) you may see what looks like the top half of a clothes hanger, minus the loop to hang with. Or you may have ropes.

The metal you obviously cannot change, but you might have a pair of pliers handy to pinch the half loop on the tops of the lamms, or the bottoms of the harnesses a bit closer if that metal V pops out now and again.

Should you have ropes, there is no problem because the chances are they are securely and correctly tied.

Evening Off Treadles—Counter-balanced or Jack Looms

When you get to the treadles themselves, you may see they are nowhere near level. This situation is easy to correct if you understand that you are just trying to make their cut ends level with each other.

How to Do It Traditionally. If you have the common garden variety of counter-balanced loom, evening off treadles is achieved with two separate pieces of strong cord. One piece is tied in a loop and snitched through the screw eye on the treadle. One piece is folded in half and snitched through a screw eye on the under side of a lamm. Then you snitch the loop over the two held together ends of the top piece of cord.

Adjust the treadle to the height you want it, and then tie an ordinary overhand knot with two ends of the top cord—as though you were *starting* to tie your shoe.

Now make sure all ties are the same degree of tautness. Believe it or not, that is all there is to it, and it will hold.

What Happens If You Don't. If you have two harnesses tied to the same treadle, but the ties are not at the same degree of tautness, you will not get a clean shed.

For example, you tie a treadle and harness 1 is fine. However, harness 4 was tied looser. Harness 1 will go down farther than harness 4. This is because you must pull the tie for harness 4 taut before it will actually go down at all.

When you are tying the treadles, tie them low enough so that you won't be trying to pull the warp through the bottom of the reed—or the top on a jack loom—when you treadle. The higher you tie treadles the wider the shed because the harnesses travel a greater distance. The effort of the warp to do what you are demanding of it will unnecessarily wear the warp.

A New Gadget Makes the Process Easier. Having said all this, let me now tell you about a marvelous little attachment that completely outdates all of the above treadle tying procedure.

There are now available tied loops of nylon cord, completely uniform in size. You pull the loop through a screw eye on the bottom of a lamm, and the knot locks it there. Next you run a long metal two-legged pin through the screw eyes on the treadle, and through the bottoms of the nylon loops. By an ingenious fluting of one leg of the long metal pin, the loop is now held to the treadle and the pin as well.

When you want to change the tie-up, you pull the pin out, which frees the loops. With today's rising costs, I refuse to quote current prices. But the last I heard was that a set of loops and pins for a four-harness loom was about $4.00. Even if it has doubled, considering the wear and tear on both your nerves and knees, the purchase seems worthwhile. And the system can be used on jack looms too—I first saw it on a jack loom and it worked perfectly.

Leveling a Jack Loom

Leveling a jack loom is simpler because there is less to adjust. Lay your string back beam to breast beam, going through a heddle and through the reed. There should be a very slight dip at the heddle because the shed is made by raising one or more harnesses, leaving the others where you now see them. The string should lie at the bottom of the reed, so that there will be room in the reed to accommodate the rising portion of the warp when you treadle.

In most jack looms that I've seen, the only real adjustment available is in the placement of the beater and the length of the cords to the treadles.

If the string does not rest on the bottom of the reed, try to find a way to raise the beater so that it will rest there. And when you are tying up the treadles beneath the lamms (if the method used is cords), remember not to tie them so high that the warp tries to jump through the top of the reed when you treadle.

The old rule was to use the smallest shed you could easily get a shuttle through. It's also easier on the warp because it is stretched less.

A Problem with Pin Tie-Up. Some looms are equipped with a pin tie-up. Each end of the pin is bent in an opposing direction and, when hooked to lamm and treadle, keeps the treadle connected to the lamm—supposedly. If you have any difficulty with this method, contact the loom maker and ask whatever questions you have. You will have to do this because there are no screw eyes to monkey around with. They have some pins differently bent, and with inserts for the holes that would be in the lamms. I don't know what their final answer to the problem is—and they may not have one yet.

Above all, do not use these looms on heavy carpets. This increases the chances of pins falling out and decreases your chances of hearing them do it. But I do guarantee you will notice the difference in your pattern after a few inches when you are minus a harness that should be tied to a certain treadle.

General Tie-Up Advice

My suggestion concerning any loom where there is a screw eye type of tie-up is to buy those two-legged pins and pre-tied loops.

Even if you can't bend down to do anything about changing the tie-ups, a small Boy Scout—or even a Cub Scout—can follow your verbal directions and get you back into business for the next project.

Checking Tie-Up Before You Weave

After you have done the tie-up, and before you start weaving, do stand at the loom and check the tie-up. Press treadle one (which we'll say should be tied to harnesses 1 and 3). When you press that treadle, do harnesses 1 and 3 rise on a jack loom or sink on a counter-balanced loom? Go on and check the next five treadles carefully, because an error found now might save you a lot of unweaving time later.

11.
Winding Shuttles and Bobbins

Winding shuttles looks as though it's an easy operation and it really is. As with many weaving procedures, the easiest method for winding shuttles is actually the best and most trouble free.

Winding Poke Shuttles

There is only one point to remember when winding wool onto any "poke" or flat shuttle; or even onto a ski shuttle, which is made of steam-bent wood with ear-like parts screwed to the top surface. Wind the shuttle so you get a small amount of slack on it; this is achieved by holding the shuttle with your fingers at a right angle to its length, and then winding over fingers and shuttle. Pull your fingers out every few rounds and repeat the procedure; this is not fussy perfection on your part at all. Wool has elasticity, and you don't want to remove it. It is part of the nature and pleasure of wool.

Making Hanks from Cones

This is why, when real perfectionists buy coned wool, they wind it into hanks, tie the beginning and finish ends together, tie the hanks in three places with a figure-eight knot, wet the hank thoroughly, and then hang to dry.

Wool on cones has been stretched to a certain degree, different degrees for different wools, and stretched wool may go back to its original length at first washing or cleaning. This is not desirable.

That figure-eight knot you tie around the hanks probably has a more esoteric name but, finished, it looks like the following. Tie the two ends of a piece of string together. Now make a half turn in about the middle of the resulting loop—you will get two almost-round loops that are connected.

Before tying your string together, figure out how to do this around your hank so that roughly half the threads are contained in one loop, and the other half in the other loop.

And when you are winding the flat (or the ski) shuttle, you get no Brownie points for winding on a whole skein of yarn; it cannot possibly go through the shed of the loom.

Particularly with smaller, or table, looms the shed is never wide enough to get a heavily loaded shuttle through. Wind the minimum and make the next one a little thicker if the first one had more than ample room in the shed. If you push a loaded shuttle through the

When winding wool, hold a poke shuttle or a ski shuttle at the middle and wind around your fingers for a few rounds. Pull out and repeat until the shuttle is wound. Your fingers have given that little bit of looseness to the winding, so the wool's elasticity is not lost. Unevenly stretched and wound wool may go back at first cleaning or washing, which would make an unattractive edge to the cloth, or give a seersucker effect in the body of the cloth. The photo is of a ski shuttle that has a projection at the top around which the yarn is wound, and has a matching "ear" at the other end of the shuttle.

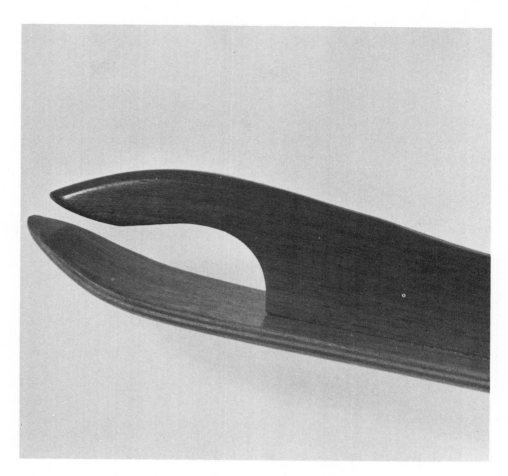

Right
*Here is a ski shuttle in profile,
so you can see just why they go
through sheds smoothly.*

Below
*Tie three figure-eight knots
around a new hank of wool to
keep it in proper order. Wet it
very thoroughly and hang it to
dry.*

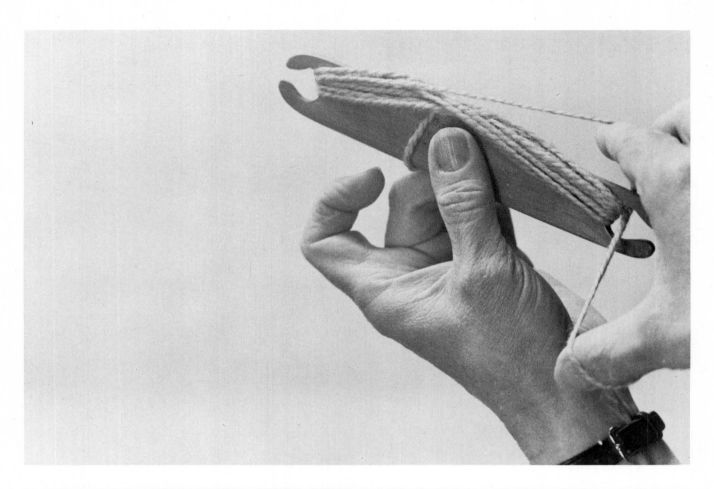

shed, the warp threads are unnecessarily fuzzed and chafed, which results in broken warp threads.

Broken warp threads are easy to mend, but why bother when you can prevent the problem?

Mending a Warp Thread

To mend a broken warp thread, first picture what you are trying to do; that is, make an extension of the actual warp thread, connecting at either end to the original warp thread, until the original thread can be brought forward and re-introduced into the weaving.

No matter where the thread breaks—in the heddle, at the fell line where the warp starts to be the woven web, or anywhere between that and the back beam—this is the way it is repaired.

Take the broken back piece of the warp and attach a new piece of the same stuff, either by a slip or a bow knot. Make sure this is done as far back as you can go—perhaps below the back beam—which will give a long end to the original thread that broke. You will need this later, when you have used up the extension piece and must butterfly the old end back into the warp, again at the fell line.

The new piece must be long enough to reach from the joining to the fell line, plus a few inches. Thread it through the correct heddle and the correct dent of the reed. It is now loose and lying on the web. Take a straight pin and poke through the web at the exact place where the new thread should go. You will know the exact place because the chances are excellent that the front end of the broken warp thread will be sticking up, or otherwise visible. Poke that broken end through to the wrong side of the web. Your pin is stuck in parallel to the beater, and brought out again to the top of the web about a quarter of an inch away. Take the new loose end you have lying on the web and fasten it around the pin.

This is done by pulling it to as close an approximation as you can tell, by your fingers, to the tension of the rest of the warp. Pull it down under one half of the pin and then up and over the other half, and down under it. Go up and over and down under the first half of the pin. Repeat this a few times, and just leave the little leftover end hanging on the web for now. When you have the weaving all finished you can weave this in with a needle so that it is almost, if not completely, hidden.

When the bow or slip knot you tied has been worked foward, by weaving and then advancing the warp, you will have to repeat the pin and tying sequence again. Be sure to check behind the heddles every so often when you think this step might be coming up. This is because a bow or slip knot can, by becoming entangled with the warp threads, cause some of them not to rise or fall in their proper places.

Winding Bobbins for a Boat Shuttle

When using a boat shuttle of any size, first a bobbin of the appropriate size must be wound and inserted.

Plastic bobbins are procurable to fit the average size shuttle, and they are most handy. Scarcely ever does the thread become twisted over the pin of the shuttle. They do have some disadvantages though, and price is one of them. A useful substitute is a plastic straw cut to a length that is proper for the given shuttle. This means to cut it as long as you can and still be able to lift the shuttle pin by pulling it up with two fingers.

There is another way to wind a poke shuttle. You can do figure-eights around the ends on the actual edge of the shuttle.

Here is the same procedure as the previous picture, but loosened and spread so you can see it better. It's good for heavy weft because you don't add the thickness of the shuttle to that of the yarn.

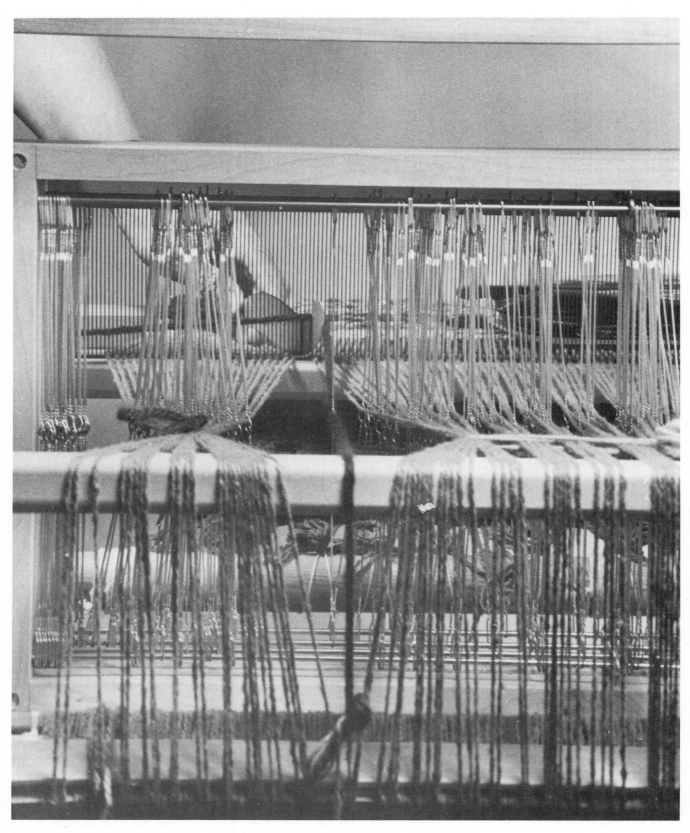

Tie the extension warp end as far back on the loom as you can get it. That will give you a good length to the old end, which you will need later on. Here the extension warp end has been tied on, put through the right heddle, and is now being put through the correct dent of the reed. Also, for that extension warp we used a much heavier and darker yarn than the rest of the warp, which was for ease of visibility in the photograph. We shall re-substitute the correct material later on.

The new end has gone through the correct heddle and the right dent of the reed. A pin or big needle has been pushed through the web at the place where the new end is to go. (If the broken end is sticking up, simply push it down through the warp.) Fasten the extension warp to the pin at the same tension as the rest of the warp, because the whole warp has to be at a uniform tension to weave off into a good cloth. Pull the extension end down under one half the pin and then up over the second half. Repeat the sequence a few times and just let the resulting tail stay where it is. The pin can come out after a few inches of weaving. The tail can be darned in after the weaving is off the loom. In this case, a light heavy yarn has been substituted to make the whole operation more clear.

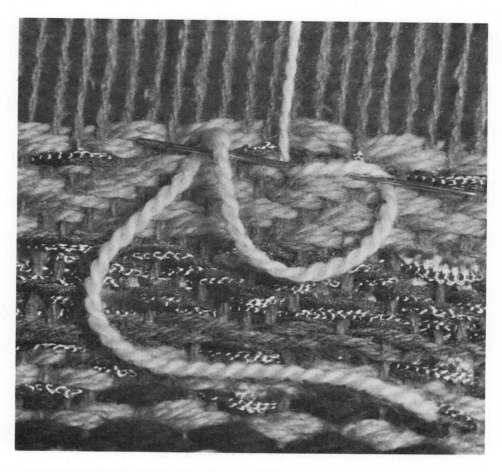

A few picks have been woven in to show how the extension warp truly becomes part of the regular warp, rising and sinking where it should. The next step, after this photograph was taken, was to substitute the correct warp material for the heavy white end—and weave it into the web along the correct path, using the white as a guide, before pulling out the white end.

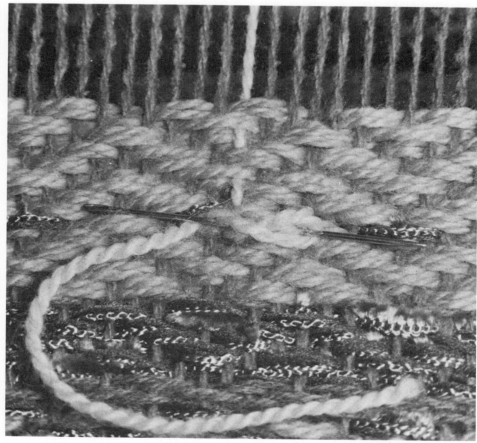

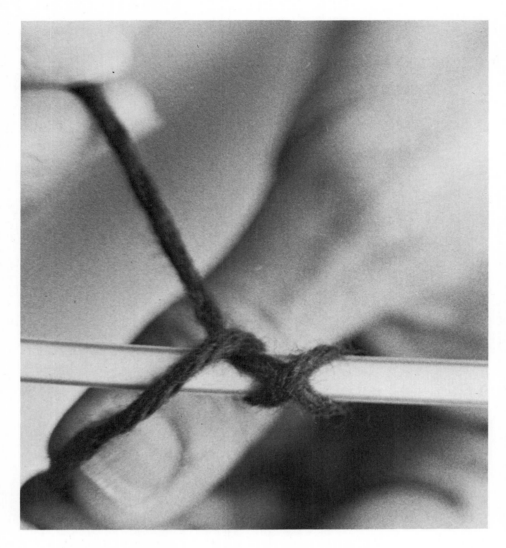

Starting to wind a plastic straw for a bobbin, you may hold the short end with your right hand, and wrap around it with the yarn in your left. Of course you may reverse hands. What shows in the photograph is what you should do because it makes the yarn stay firm on the bobbin without knotting.

Below
Then wind a small knob at each end and fill in between them. Repeat the knobs closer to center, and fill in between them. This is so that the knobs won't fall off the ends of the bobbin and tangle in the shuttle.

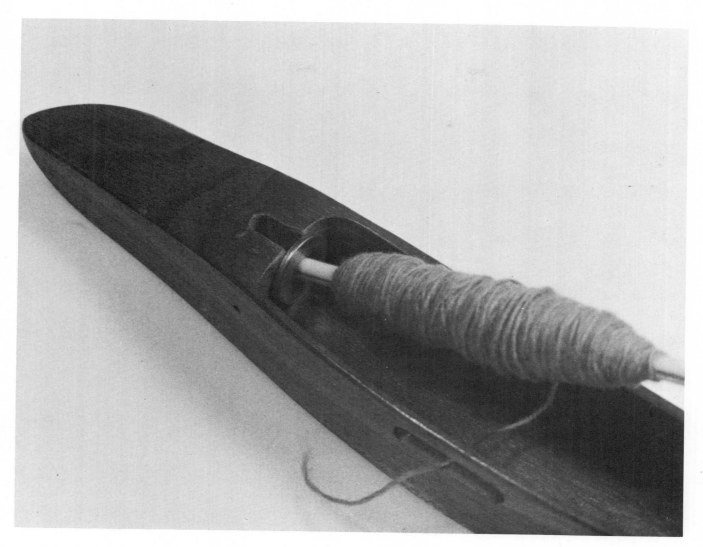

A thick washer was put on the pin of this shuttle before the bobbin, to prevent the end of the straw binding against the pin's hinging system. Note that a bobbin always goes into a boat shuttle so that the weft feeds through the slot in the side from underneath.

Make sure the straw diameter is large enough to go on the shuttle pin. Our luxurious supermarket stocks two sizes of straws—one works and one does not.

Straws must be wound more carefully than the plastic bobbins or loops fly off the ends and get tangled, as mentioned above.

How to Wind. The winding procedure is simple. Wind a sort of knob at one end and one at the other end, and then fill in between; repeat a little closer to the center until the bobbin is comfortably full. This is for the electric or the manual winder.

Not Too Full and Why. Comfortably full, in this case, is rather like the after-dinner feeling. Only here it is the bobbin that has to be able to move around. Never wind a bobbin so full it will not rotate on the spindle pin of the shuttle. It is not wrong, but it is a distinct nuisance. It is also a very easy way to break selvedge threads of a fine wide warp, which should make you remember not to do it—after you have done it once.

Some shuttles will give you problems where the bobbin rests against the hinge assembly of the shuttle's pin. This is easily fixed by putting a thick washer on the spindle before you put the bobbin on. A washer, in case you are not a mechanical type of person, looks like a well-licked Lifesaver candy, but is made of metal.

Electric Bobbin Winder vs Manual

There is a lot of discussion about electric versus manual bobbin winders, and I suppose there will be more before we are all through weaving. To many of us, the discussion is finished when we discover that electric models are about twice the price of the manual ones.

Electric winders have a strong advantage if you weave a lot with fine threads. Obviously you will save time and perhaps avoid a stiff elbow by using one.

In a conversation I heard about a month ago, a point was raised that had not occurred to me. One weaver said she never used her electric winder for wool because it winds the bobbins too tight. It is quite true that the electric winder gives a firmer bobbin, with more yardage per bobbin, than the manual style. But I had not considered that here was a far from obvious way to remove wool's natural elasticity.

This would be particularly true if you had a good supply of bobbins, either the plastic style or straw, and decided to make up 40 or so, and then didn't get to the actual weaving for a week. A fair analogy would be to imagine your hair up in rollers for a week.

I make no recommendations here at all, realizing personal preference is always personal preference. I am simply relaying points and opinions about both types. It is up to you to make the decision.

How a Bobbin Is Inserted in the Shuttle. Do make a mental note that when you put a bobbin into a shuttle, you must do it so that the thread always feeds from *under* the bobbin. I have never heard of any exception—always, always, always do this.

A really wet washcloth laid over a linen warp in this fashion will dampen the cloth and warp rapidly and efficiently. And no, this is not *a linen warp, but it is the way to lay the washcloth, half over the warp and half over the cloth.*

Wind Linen Dry, but Use It Wet

There is one point about bobbins that I hesitate to mention because the authorities don't mention it, and I have been laughed at. But since it works for me, you may want to try it out. Somewhere I read that—and this is a direct quote—"you weave linen wet." Perhaps because my first boss was an efficiency expert, I tend to look for the easy way in any area of endeavor.

Fact: I was told to weave linen wet. Fact: I have dried something like umpteen million dishes in my long and checkered career, mostly with linen dish towels. Fact: I therefore know linen absorbs moisture quicker than a Kansas lawn on a hot day. Fact: it doesn't strike me as sensible to try to get a warp soaking wet when that warp is on a wooden loom. Deduction: get the *bobbins* soaking wet, and capillary attraction will take care of the warp after the first couple of picks. Action: wind a handful of bobbins the night before you plan to weave linen, and stand them in a coffee mug of water overnight. When you are down to about half a mug of bobbins during the weaving, change the water, wind another half a mug of bobbins, and go back to the weaving.

But Don't Forget, the Warp Must Be Wet. Two additional notes should be made here. The warp must be quite damp before you start using the wet bobbin. If not, there will be a difference in the cloth woven with the wet bobbins on dry warp and the cloth woven on warp made wet by the use of wet bobbins. An almost soaking-wet washcloth is laid on the unwoven warp at about the fell line. Let it stay for the length of time it takes to pick a bunch of flowers, finish your tea, or write a postcard.

Prevent the Stench. The second note, should you find your bobbins all nice and wet the next morning, but have a change of plans on your calendar: take those bobbins out of the water. If it is winter, put them on the heat to dry. If it is summer, lay them on a sunny windowsill. You would not believe the smell of linen-wound bobbins left too long in water.

12.
What Shall I Weave?

Contrary to your logical reasoning about this chapter title, what follows will not be a recipe section. I shall not tell you that blank ends per inch, blank inches wide, with certain threads, will give you a poncho, guest towel, wall hanging, or even table cloth.

What I am trying to do is let you discover what you might want to weave. This is not quite the same as letting you discover the wheel in the first year of engineering school, though it may appear so.

If we can now assume you know how to make and beam a warp, and can intelligently read a book on weaving, there is practically nothing you are likely to want to do now that is beyond you. The knowledge of a technique, the width of your loom, and the number of harnesses on it are your limitations.

Experience is a very secondary limitation; although it is obvious that weaving with fine linen, when all you have used previously is carpet warp, presents problems. However, if you want to weave with very fine linen, and are prepared for the frustrations and broken warps that are fairly predictable with a new weaver, why not?

I had a student not so long ago who turned out a lovely linen wall hanging of zingy Scandinavian yellows, oranges, and reds. Her previous experience? One knitting worsted scarf. Number of broken warp threads? Two. Not only that, she is exceptionally pretty and has great charm, which goes to show that some people are more than fairly blessed.

Questions to Ask Yourself

What to weave is such a personal matter that you should, I think, figure out who you are, what you enjoy doing, what annoys you about this new hobby, what your favorite aspects of it are, and then think about all your answers to evolve your own approach. Not to be neglected here are your own personal limitations: money, interrupted (or uninterrupted) time, physical mobility, etc.

Budget

If you are financially limited, you might want to consider doing weavings that require cheap material, but need skill or time. Double woven hot mats for your friends at Christmas, on a vari-colored linen warp (because you ran into a yarn sale of linens, but only a bit of each) might be your answer.

Spectacle cases also done in the double weave and stuffed with Dacron batting for all the Christmas list will surely keep you busy for a while. If your list is long but your loom is a table model, remember to cut some of the woven cases off before they pile up so much on the front roller that you cannot fit any more under the breast beam.

A needlework bag of nylon or cotton can be woven for your friend who carefully does beautiful needlework, but who also throws her bag into the back of the car, with the kids, groceries, and the lawnmower on its way to the repairman! Had you more money, or a more careful friend, you could make a wool bag, but the nylon or cotton one dives happily into her overworked washing machine.

If you are really scraping bottom with the yarn budget, a bathroom or kitchen window "blind" made of nylon, cotton, or linen warp, with sliced up cleaners' bags for weft is terrific. The occasional printing on these bags comes out as flecks of color and adds even more sparkle and shimmer. You wash them by zipping them through a sink full of dish detergent and water, and hang them right back up again. A real drip-dry article. Cut the weft-to-be strips about a third of an inch in width and they act like yarn, but cut wider the effect can be of little puffs of sparkle.

Time, Lots or Little?

If lack of time is your only problem, you might do as a pretty young doctor does. She is determined to weave, in spite of the responsibilities connected with a husband, small children, and a house—as well as the clinic. Her warps are coarse—I don't think she has ever had a sett of more than 10 epi—the wefts are heavy and patterns simple. But her gaudy pillows delight the small son with vision problems, all the relatives have scarves in their pet colors, and every bed in her house has a handwoven afghan at the foot.

There is always the chance of the opposite problem with time. What if you have too much of it to match your budget—which means you weave faster than you can accumulate threads money. Why not change your weavings to things that are very time consuming? A telephone book cover with a tapestry inlaid cover, guitar straps in a very complicated Finnvav, a bound weave tote bag? These fairly simple projects could use up a normal person's spare time for a year.

When I arrange the time for my next project, it will be clothes for a beautiful old doll. Researching for her appropriate costume would be time pleasantly spent. This won't be a hurry-up project at all, but the reading, the considering, the planning, and the weaving should be as much fun as the equivalent time spent at bingo. I never won at bingo anyway—the one time I played it.

A woman I know is doing a wall hanging for a paneled wall, on which she says all pictures look simply awful. She looked at that wall for two years, hung up skeins of colored yarn on a wire clothes hanger to get the family's reactions, progressed to hanging samples, and is now doing the wall hanging itself. It is being woven quite open, so that the 18th century paneling will show through. The colors she finally chose are those of the couch and the curtains combined.

The lesson in the previous two paragraphs is—you do not have to hurry. A hobby is not a time limit exam. It is to be savored like a Rembrandt etching, a beautiful view, or a real strawberry sundae.

Of Time, Budget, Interest, and Philosophy

One of my seldom seen but much loved friends is a very old farm woman. She lives in a beautiful old house and manages on a minuscule pension. When I asked her last summer what she was weaving, I was given a marvelous answer.

"Now that I have the time I am sorting out my old samples and weaving dollhouse rugs for my great-granddaughters."

Knowing her weavings fairly well, I can imagine the museum quality of those rugs. And knowing her affection for fine linens, I realize perfectly that she is using her old samples because she cannot afford linen. But pity has no place here because she is doing what she enjoys for those whom she loves. How many of us do better?

Interest. This is a heading that I would very much like to have in red, surrounded on all four sides with exclamation points. Anything at all so that you will stop and consider the whole section well.

There is absolutely no reason to weave overshot projects if you do not like the weave. You are not going to heaven faster if you weave with plum because it is the fashion, but you loathe all variations in that color range.

Just because the medium is weaving, which you like, do not expect your previous prejudices to dissolve magically.

Take what you do like in this new hobby and build from there. If you like tying together disparate color elements in a room, do it with wall hangings, pillows, or table mats—depending on the room. If your sense of humor is subtle, and the dog always sleeps on the couch, put his name on the pillows, not the family initial.

If you like experimenting and don't want to end up with a shelf-full of sample books, find someone who dresses dolls and let her have your trial pieces. Should you be the sort who enjoys reading one book slowly through the winter, reveling in footnotes, looking up unfamiliar words for the precise meanings, make yourself a tapestry bookmark.

What I am trying to get you to do is think about *you*, what type of person you are, what your enjoyments are, what sort of activities give you pleasure, and then translate them into weaving projects.

Now, will you please do me a favor and go back—right now—to the heading *Interest* and re-read back to this point?

Purpose. This is a once-over-lightly heading, a sort of review before any project is started. Do let your project fit its intended use, please.

Let a scarf for a little girl be a reasonable length for her, a sensible width, and a suitable weave and material.

Too many people forget that just because a thing is handwoven, it does not automatically mean it's of value.

Lengths of tweed should have a good "hand"—that indefinable quality that makes them tailor and walk well.

Wall hangings should not be fuzzy and impossible to clean for someone who lives in a dirty section of the country—and has no air conditioner.

Ask yourself what is going to happen to your project? Isn't a jolly pink toy cat, woven in nylon, stuffed with Dacron, and embroidered with cotton, more practical than one woven in wool, cotton stuffed, and the "embroidery" done with a marking pen?

Ask yourself how will this project stand up to what is expected of it?

And repeat your answer out loud three times before you *do* any project. Success is a lot more likely to follow.

Winding Multi-Color Warps

Getting really specific, here are two hints for those woven belts mentioned a while back that deserve an individual heading because they enormously improve the belts.

First, if you have seven yarns you want to use together in a belt, choose a pattern with a seven thread repeat; with nine yarns, a nine thread repeat.

Second, do not choose a pattern requiring a tabby. Usually tabby shots match the warp, to get the most out of a given pattern; and if your warp is nine colors, you can see difficulties approaching faster than an Oklahoma tornado. The various bird's eye and rosepath threadings can be exciting and brilliant here. If your mood is different, beiges and ivories, which are almost but not quite identical, can't be topped for sophistication.

How to Wind. When you wind these warps, wind one color end front to back of the warp on the frame; then cut off and tie the next color on very securely to it. Wind that back to the front of the warp; cut it off and tie on the next. Wind that like the first—front of the warp to the back—and keep on doing this for the whole warp. It is an infuriatingly time-consuming operation, but if you have wound enough warp for two or three belts and then used a different color weft for each belt, your annoyance will diminish somewhat.

Notes to Make. If you put your color order on a piece of paper, with samples of each color attached, and tape it above the warping frame, your problems will diminish in this area too.

If you become really enamored of this sort of warp, learn to use a warping paddle. Have someone show you how, because trying to learn from a book or from pictures is like trying to learn how to ride a bicycle from slides. I have never read what I consider adequate directions, nor could I write them out.

Mohair Scarves, Stoles, and Etceteras

If your free time is really limited, and you live in an occasionally chilly part of the world, mohair is your all purpose answer to gift problems.

Sett for the Mohair Projects. Don't use more than five ends to the inch. Using more is not wrong, but the resulting problems are that the mohair warp will stick to itself and no shed will happen at all if you insist upon disregarding this advice.

The Time It Takes. Now for the good news. Yes, the stuff is expensive, but you use very little yardage. A stole may take you an evening or two to weave. A scarf will take no longer than one TV special. You never really beat in mohair weft—you use the beater to press the weft into a straight line. If you do slam the beater by mistake, unweave the slammed wefts carefully and re-weave.

Other Projects to Consider

Wool scarves are the answer for men and little boys too. A scarf that is really long enough for the uncle who is six feet five will be a total success, particularly if the colors go with his favorite topcoat. A small boy's scarf with his initials picked up in color at one end is more fun than the mundane name tapes, and less likely to get lost too.

A stack of linen warp, cotton flake weft guest towels is a luxurious present for your millionaire friend—or your other friend who hates ironing. And it is not bad for a wedding present either. They wash, dry in the machine, fold, and then stack.

Pillows are for the rich weaver who will use hand-spun or hand-dyed wools as well as for the economical weaver who will use acrylic and other man-mades in colors that will complement particular rooms. They are for the limited free time weaver who will use the coarse yarns, easy patterns, and rely on the color and textured patterns for effect—as with the pretty young doctor. But they also work for the weaver who will do elaborate, time consuming pickup work—like slicing old fur jackets (out-of-doors) into thin strips and placing the resulting wefts very carefully.

A rug for an awkwardly shaped hall can be expensive or cheap, time consuming or very quick. How about a litterbag cover for the car, or a car robe to match the upholstery or the car color? Or perhaps a giant bright linen bath towel for the sun worshipper you know?

And don't forget the whimsies that eat up time greedily, but are a delight to make. I don't think I've ever met one child who wouldn't be thrilled with a bright green, honeycomb weave dragon. A Christmas tree skirt of deep greens with picked up embroidery weave snowflakes and stars could go to your "But They Have Everything" friends.

There is really something for everybody lurking in your loom, and all you have to do is figure what it is and for whom.

Table Looms for the Physically Handicapped

If you are physically limited—a touch of arthritis or a temporary cast, etc.—and thus don't want to get down under a loom, you should consider a table loom. True, they take longer to weave on, but you don't end up under them.

Some companies are importing wider looms from Scandinavia than I am used to seeing produced here. Another thing, that great Vermont loom maker who makes my looms is making multi-harness for a slight extra charge!

I have heard of people exchanging floor looms for table looms. A long time weaver with hip problems exchanged her floor loom for a college girl's table loom. The older woman could no longer get down to change the tie-ups that she liked to do frequently, and the young girl didn't have the cash to buy a floor loom. Probably the younger one made out better dollarwise, but I notice the ex-floor loom owner has a very tidy studio these days—and I am sure she didn't tidy it herself.

Off-Beat Projects

One year when our daughter was going to be away for Christmas, I wove a long red ribbon tie, cut a few variegated holly branches from the bush in our yard, tied on the bow, and laid it on the top of her Christmas present. Judging from her thank-you letter, you can't tell me the young are not sentimental.

When my mother was in a wheelchair, I wove her a lap blanket in her favorite colors in the width she wanted that was narrow enough so the fringes would not catch in the wheels.

A friend has a real Georgian dining room table, 9¼ feet (3.8 m) long. Thanks to my loom, she now has a 9 inch (23 cm) wide holiday runner of 16/1 linen, the length of the table plus an extra 1 foot (30.5

cm) drop at either end. It matches exactly the gold in her dining room wallpaper, and looks marvelous over the Irish damask cloths.

What about handwoven articles for the other craftspeople—or the knitters or sewers? A case for knitting needles can be an heirloom piece. Even an ordinary needle case for the sewing cabinet can be fine and lovely, particularly when teamed with a matching pincushion. A wall hanging for the kitchen, with double weave pockets here and there, planned to fit wooden spoons—with the wooden spoons included in the wall hanging—is a real winner.

If the church group catches you in a weak moment and you volunteer something for the handcrafts table, you might consider the following possibilities. Shoulder tote bags scaled for little girls; pincushions from some of your sample warps; carriage blankets in machine-washable yarns; bright belts and sashes—even boys wear them in my area of the country. You might make some coin snap purses to slide onto the belts too.

A blanket of handspun yarn, even for a child, will eat up the grocery money in a hurry. But a 2 inch square checkerboard for her dollhouse may take 10¢ worth of 20/2 cotton at the most. And who is to say what is more fun to do, or more appealing to the recipient? My brother has a green Swedish wool scarf in the same yarn as his favorite pullover. I know it is the same yarn, because I knit the pullover.

Now these all are really enjoyable types of weaving, interesting problems, interesting solutions, and good conversation pieces. But you will not find the "recipes" in any books on weaving that I have run across. These are the projects that require imagination, a tape measure, and a lot more thinking time than warping frame or loom time.

There now, do you have enough suggestions to go off and have your own off-beat ideas? I thought so.

Basic "In Stock" Yarns to Have

There are various schools of thought on what yarns you should have "in stock" at all times. My own feeling is never to buy colors you really loathe or textures you do not find appealing. Going farther than that becomes mostly a matter of opinion.

What You Really Need . . . When I first started to weave, I was told that a minimum stock of yarns would be $1,000.00. With two children rapidly approaching the college years, I quickly moved the decimal point over one place—as the maximum. When you get right down to it, if you have enough threads to do the next project, you have enough stock. I think if more of us realized this fact, we would be happier— and have more storage space as well.

Christmas Comes Every Year . . .

Christmas presents can come rolling off your loom in great abundance. A long warp in a reasonably neutral color—and with different wefts suited to the rooms—will make pillows for your favorite people, as I mentioned previously. But it could make tote bags or book covers just as easily, using the same approach.

This year might be the year of the potholder. With a very long warp, that Dacron batt material for filling, and a little hand quilting (or machine quilting if December 25 is approaching fast), and you are well on the road. If your good neighbor has just bought a poppy colored stove, matching linen potholders would be appreciated—and they would last and last.

A scarf to match a sweater is a good idea for your knitting—but not weaving—friend as it was for my non-weaving brother.

Chair seats, pincushions, bookcovers, a piece of hand woven linen for your embroidery minded friend, blinds for your own kitchen window, cloth to cover a speaker for the hi-fi system, a bathmat small enough to fit a very small bathroom, a baby blanket, a machine-washable yellow car robe for your young friend who just bought a new yellow sports car.

With all the above notions, we have not even mentioned table runners in wild colors, place mats to go with the family dishes, lengths of skirt material, coverlets for the beds, or throw blankets to match—or contrast with—the rooms they were planned for.

One year I gathered up all the old Christmas ribbons, bells, and bows at the end of my friend's holiday party. "May I have these?" I asked. "Be my guest," she said. The next Christmas I took her a wall hanging in which the articles were used in various ways. I didn't really like it as a wall hanging, but she did and that is what matters.

Don't Forget the Dollhouse

Should there be a dollhouse on your visiting list, you have a hobby forever. Everything from infinitesimal wall hangings mounted on sanded cocktail toothpicks to fine woven wall "paper" and everything in between—rugs, floor cushions, a tiny checkerboard, overshot coverlets, curtains and a "rag" stair carpet can be made from your out-of-date samples.

In other words, use everybody's ideas, plus your loom, plus your yarns, plus your own point of view, to come up with your own individual weavings.

13.
Weaving

Just to show you there are many types of weavers, one weaver confessed to me, "I really don't enjoy the actual weaving too much. Making all the samples, working with graph paper, getting the big warp ready—all that is great—but the weaving is so anticlimactic."

Whether or not you will look at it that way, I don't know, but now is the time to discuss the anticlimactic part.

The warp is ready to be woven on—beamed, threaded, sleyed, tied on; the tentative tie-up has been made, you have an hour or two of free time ahead and a smile on your face.

How to Turn the Front Bundles to a Warp
There are several ways to turn the row of bundles that you tied on at the front of the loom into a real warp, and you should use the one you like best.

Shed Sticks. You could put in shed sticks, which are just laths procurable at the lumber yard. Have them cut long enough so that they will just roll onto the front beam. And be sure to measure the exact length you need at both the cloth and warp beams. On some looms there is up to an inch difference—the larger measure usually being at the back, but don't count on it.

Shed sticks are put in by first treadling one tabby, laying the stick in on that shed, changing sheds to the opposite tabby, beating, and then laying in another stick on the new tabby, making sure the sticks are absolutely centered on the warp. If you miss this step, you will skew your warp later on when you are rolling those sticks onto the cloth beam. Probably four sticks total will make those bundles into a correctly spaced warp.

Correcting a Threading Error. One big advantage to the sticks is the ease with which you can see a possible threading error. They work like a magnifying glass; and now is the ideal time to correct any errors. You cut—or untie—the bundle containing the offending end at the front, pull it out and replace on the right harness with a string heddle.

By Helper Heddle. Or use a purchased "helper heddle" (or whatever your supply man calls them). This is the heddle that hooks over the top and bottom heddle bars of the correct harness. When the warp end is in the correct position, you tie it again to the front with the rest of the ends. When you are doing this, make certain that you go

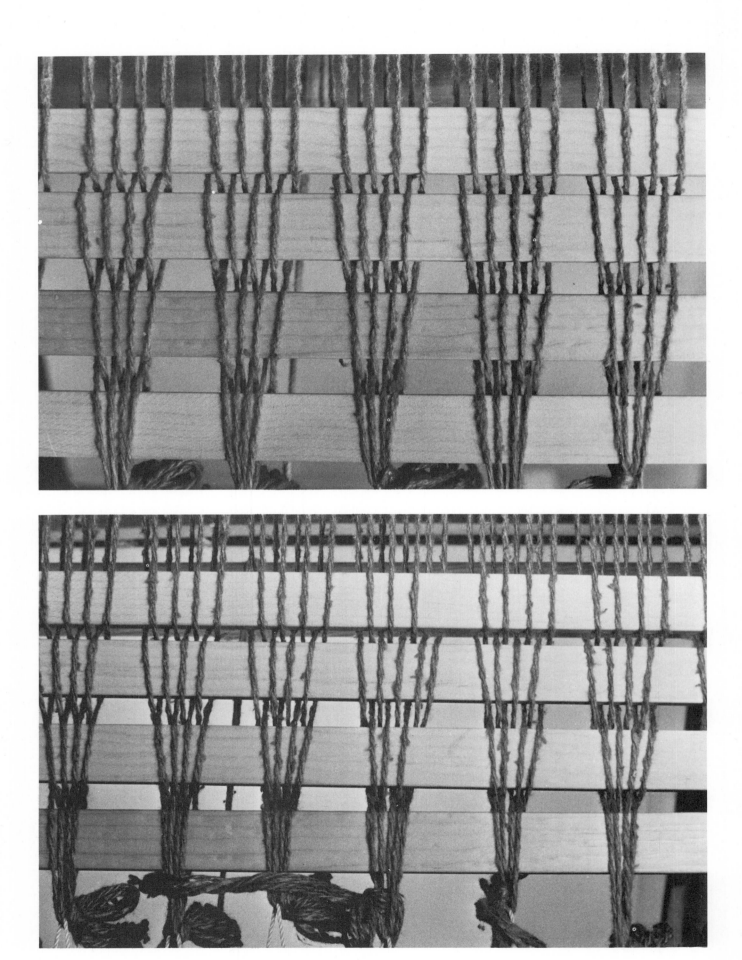

through the right dent of the reed and that the tension is close to the tension on the rest of the warp.

If the tension is noticeably tighter, that end will soon snap. If it is noticeably looser, it may take longer to snap; but it will saw and rub and—I promise you—eventually snap.

Rags or Sliced Up Stockings. You can also use evenly cut-width fine rags at the beginning to turn those bundles into a warp; or old stockings that you have sliced. The same tabby treadling method holds true. And be sure to check for threading errors with this method too—or with any method.

Bobbins. To bring the warp bouts or bundles into a smooth warp, my usual method is a fine way to use up old bobbins of this and that. Try to concentrate on the fairly sticky ones, because I feel they do the job faster than the slick cottons or smooth artificial fibers.

As with many of my recommendations, this one also has an exception. Should you be making something in which the whole warp will show on the finished piece—a wall hanging, a stole—take up the extra inch or so of warp it will require and use a contrasting color smooth weft for the beginning. The smooth weft will take longer to achieve a warp from bundles, but it is much safer because it is easier to pick out later on when you are finishing your article.

Weave In Any of These Wefts by Tabbies. There are probably many other ways to start a warp, but one I find very easy is to treadle tabby A (13), pass the shuttle through the shed, then tabby B (24), pass the shuttle through that shed, repeat tabby A, pass the shuttle through and then—and not until then—beat with the beater. Sometimes only two repetitions of this sequence will properly space the warp.

It is the shortest weaving length I know that will turn those bundles into a warp and, if your warp is a skimpy length anyway (because you did your warp figuring math and found you could barely make it with what you had), you might like to try this method first.

Selvedges—Their Importance or Unimportance
On the subject of selvedges there are two schools of thought. One says smooth selvedges are the mark of a good weaver; when making wall hangings and stoles, I completely agree. However, on a piece of yard goods that will be cut and where the selvedges will never be seen, it seems rather like ironing your cleaning rags before you use them. But if good selvedges make you happy, by all means take the time to do them. You surely should know how to make them at will—I do agree with the good selvedge school on that.

Weaving Rhythm, How to Develop One
Rhythm in weaving will be achieved in many cases if the bobbins are well wound. And the gaining of rhythm is achieved not only by your hands, but your feet as well. If you have your treadles tied up so that you treadle left-right on the outside treadles, then left-right on the inner ones—but if you are a one-two-three-six-five-four person, you will never get any rhythm to it.

You might just as well get down under that loom and retie your treadles now. Whether you are starting on a 10 yard (9.1 m) warp or a 5 foot (1.5 m) scarf, the weaving will be no pleasure if the treadling is not your style.

Lay in and center a stick on one tabby shed. Beat. Lay in and center a stick on the opposite tabby shed. Beat. Continue laying in sticks on alternate tabby sheds and beating, until the bundles become a correctly spaced warp.

On first glance, this appears to be a duplicate of the previous picture, but look again and you should see a threading error. The wrong end will be identified and untied at the front of the warp. It will then have to be unsleyed, unthreaded—and then correctly re-threaded, resleyed, and tied again at the front. This means you must put in either a helper heddle or make a string heddle on the correct harness, and in the correct place.

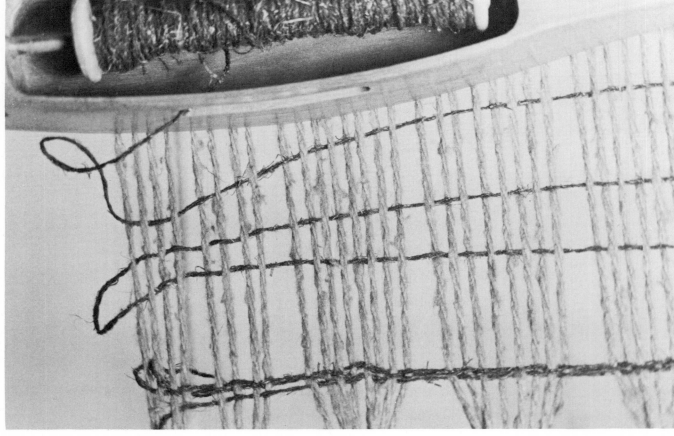

The Advantages of Ski Shuttles

If your warp is wide and your weft is quite heavy, the praises of ski shuttles cannot be sung too loudly. A little paste wax on the under side of a ski shuttle rubbed up with an old bit of fine steel wool or real wool, and they really float through a shed. The prices may look like a luxury, but if you are at all biased in favor of heavy weft they are a necessary delight.

Another point in their favor is the ease with which they enter a warp. Unlike a flat poke shuttle that—by the very nature of its name must be poked through the shed, the ski shuttle will glide through after the initial thrust and is a lot easier on selvedge threads.

Starting the First Weft

Starting the first shuttle of the weft, you go through left-to-right ordinarily, and leave a 2-or-3 inch tail hanging. Wrap that over the first warp end and lay it back into the same shed, then bring it to the top surface of the warp a few ends later. It can be cut after a few picks, preferably with a pair of curved bandage scissors, so you don't cut any other wefts or warps.

Joining New Wefts

Joining in a new weft can either be done at the selvedge or in the middle of the warp. For you beautiful selvedge buffs, you had better do it in the middle. On a fragile wall hanging join the weft at the selvedge please, so the join does not show. A constant joining in of new wefts at one selvedge or the other will eventually give you a build up, if the weft is even moderately heavy, so remember there are both left and right hand selvedges.

Joining new weft in the middle of the warp is done by overlapping for a few warp ends. The tail of old weft can be brought to the top surface and, if you are weaving from right to left, the tail of the new weft may come up a few ends to its right. Obviously, if the joining is made on a left-to-right shed, the old weft comes to the top surface and the new one a few warp ends to its left.

You do not try to pop the shuttle down through the top layer of warp to do all this. You shoot the new shuttle through, in the same direction as the one you ran out of, and reach between a pair of warp threads in the general area where you want the new tail to appear. Next pull up to the top surface the beginning of that shuttle's weft, which is then the new tail.

Steps in the Act of Weaving: Throw, Beat, Change

There is a lot of controversy about the actual act of weaving. One teacher told me to throw, then beat and change sheds simultaneously. And she was a very good teacher. Some will say to throw, beat, and then change sheds. Some wefts you will use will work best if you throw, beat, change sheds, then beat again. If you have problems, try to get advice from weavers who have used whatever esoteric wefts you are attempting.

If that is not available, sit down and experiment, using your common sense. You will probably learn more that way.

Variations in the Steps. For instance, if you are throwing, then beating and changing sheds simultaneously, but the weft is not being placed to your liking, or is not staying in place but seems to creep up toward the reed, something is wrong. You could try the throw, beat, *then*

Pass shuttle through shed for Tabby A. Repeat in Tabby B shed. Repeat in Tabby A shed.

When you have finished the previous step, only then do you beat. Repeat the sequence— using Tabby B, Tabby A, Tabby B, then beating. Leave loops at the selvedges and these shots will be even easier to take out later. Many times these six picks will turn the warp bundles to a warp—but if not, try another few picks.

After the bundles have become a warp, you will want to start the ''real'' weft. Open the first shed that the pattern calls for, shoot the shuttle through, left to right, leaving a tail at the left-hand selvedge. Now wrap the tail around the selvedge warp end; lay it into that shed for an inch or so to the right and then bring it to the top surface. Beat the weft into place and, after a few picks, you may cut it—preferably with round pointed, curved blade bandage scissors. These scissors lessen the chances of cutting other warps and wefts unintentionally, so they are almost in the class of necessities.

change shed, *then* beat again routine, and see if that helps. Or you might wet your bobbins very thoroughly.

The point to bear in mind at any step of the weaving process is: hysterics will not help. They are necessary only if the house is burning down and the firemen don't know how to fold your loom to get it out through the door.

Weaving is a remarkably simple process that has been refined through thousands of years and minds, and most of the answers are in the literature or in your head. Perhaps both.

Preventing Selvedge Loops When Colors Change
If you have color changes to make and the pattern permits you to do this at the selvedges, it is easier. If they come often, then lock in the unused color or colors at the selvedges every few picks to avoid long loops at those selvedges. If you will practice this, you will find that the first pick you do with a newly picked up and seldom used shuttle lies in the shed better, and the selvedges are better too.

Locking in an unused color so that there will be no long loop at the selvedge is done by laying the shuttle you are using in above the unused color, or under it, in order that the unused thread will somehow get caught into the web before the pick is made.

Optimum Length for Flat Shuttles
When using poke, flat, or rug shuttles—all these names are used for the flat shuttles with a half O cut out of each end—make sure they are at least as long as the warp is wide. If they aren't, I guarantee you the selvedge threads will be sawed and fuzzed where you push the shuttle

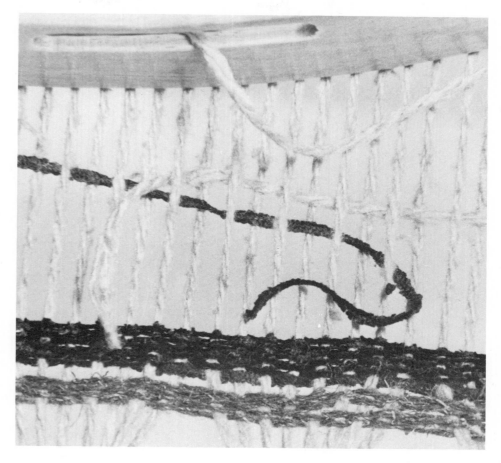

Joining on new wefts requires an overlap of a few ends. Here is how to get it. Bring the last bit of yarn to the top surface; shoot a new full shuttle through in the same direction, from the selvedge. If you were going to the right from left, reach down and pull the new weft tail up a few ends to the left of where the old tail appears. Remember to do all this in reverse if your old shuttle direction was right to left. Different colors of weft were used here for clarity only. Color changes would tend to happen at a selvedge.

Of course you've read the preceding caption carefully and started your full shuttle at the selvedge. You have not tried to put that shuttle down into the middle of the warp. Had you done that, you could break some warp threads quite easily. Reach down into the shed between a pair of warps in the general area where you want the new tail to appear, and pull the new warp tail up to the surface.

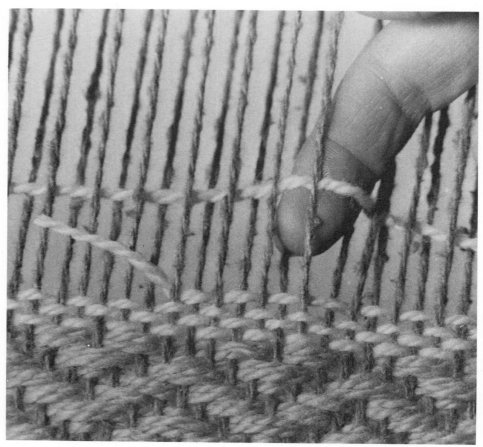

Lock in seldom used wefts at the selvedges every few picks, if neat selvedges matter to you. Skip this step, and your selvedges will appear as they do here. And another thing, if you will lock in the wefts, the seldom used ones lie better in the shed when they do appear. In this photo, it does not even get into the shed for about three or four ends from the selvedge. This is another example of what happens if you persist in breaking old rules for no good reason.

Catching in a rarely used shuttle so that there will be no long loop between its appearances means hooking it over or under (at the selvedge every few picks) the yarn you mainly use. Remembering to do this will also prevent the selvedge thread not being caught and thus not being covered, as is shown in the photo just above the long loop at the selvedge. Experiment here to get a rhythm to this step, as you will do in so many other aspects of the weaving process.

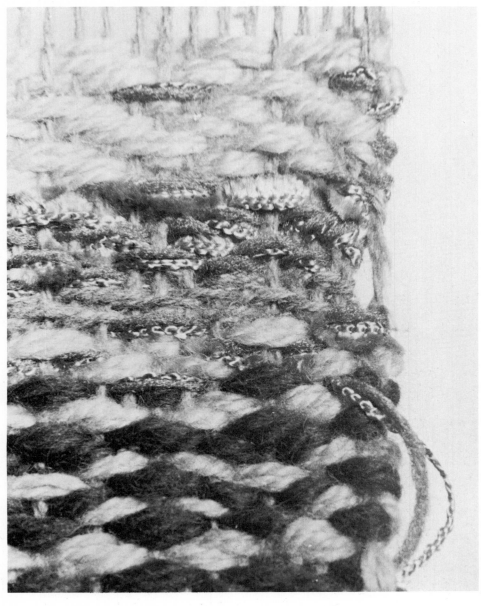

through the shed, or where you reach in at one selvedge to retrieve it. If you do not have shuttles long enough to avoid this, push the shuttle through very close to the reed where the shed is largest, and do the whole process carefully.

Throwing Boat Shuttles
Shooting a boat shuttle through a shed seems to have a certain mystique attached to it, which I find bewildering.

You Do This . . .Hold the shuttle in the palm of either hand, with the hole (or slot) through which the weft feeds, toward you. Try to get your index finger at one end to help give it a shove. Shoot it through the shed with enough force to get it all the way through, so you can catch it with the other hand.

Try to catch it with your thumb on the top of the bobbin in the shuttle. This is not as arbitrary and meaningless a direction as it may seem.

And the Shuttle Does This . . . By so doing, you are preventing that bobbin from continuing its spinning action, which carried the weft off during its travel through the shed. With a wide warp and a wiry linen or artificial thread, forgetting this can ruin your temper.

The weft unwinds from the bobbin but—because the shuttle has stopped—has no place to go, so it all tangles inside the shuttle. Not to be recommended at all.

Remedying an Uncatching Selvedge End
While weaving you may notice that one thread at each selvedge does not catch. The following remedy often works. However, there will be no lengthy explanation of why because it will be easier for you to try it out; watch the rising and sinking of the warp threads, and try to understand it that way. If your sequence is:

> Shed A, R to L
> Shed B, L to R
> Shed C, R to L
> Shed D, L to R

cut your weft and start at the opposite selvedge, but continue in the proper ABCD sequence. No matter at what letter shed you stopped, continue with the next letter. A table of the new sequence will now appear thusly:

> Shed A, L to R
> Shed B, R to L
> Shed C, L to R
> Shed D, R to L

If only one selvedge thread does not catch, try the above remedy for this case as well. If you still have one selvedge thread that does not catch, cut it, take it back—way back—to the back beam, so that it will not get enmeshed with its neighbors.

Retying Treadles to Your Liking
Once you have your shuttles under control and have decided how you want your treadles tied for this project, you would be wise to make a little treadling sheet (like the threading sheet) and tape it to your loom at a comfortable reading height.

If you have a four-harness loom, either jack or counter-balance, this will consist of a combination of no more than the numbers from one to six, because that is the maximum number of treadles these looms have. It may read:

1
2
1
6
5
6

which has absolutely nothing to do with the harnesses. To reinforce this point, you might write it so:

Treadles
1
2
1
6
5
6

And you have achieved these numbers by the following method. The treadling directions in the book you are using said:

Treadle 1 activating harnesses 12
Treadle 2 activating harnesses 23
Treadle 3 activating harnesses 12
Treadle 4 activating harnesses 34
Treadle 5 activating harnesses 14
Treadle 6 activating harnesses 34

But you decided that using treadle one and then two and then three with the left foot, and four and then five and then six with the right foot is not your style. You prefer to use:

1
2
1
6
5
6

So you must tie the harnesses in a fashion that permits you to treadle as you wish, but activates the harnesses as the book decrees to get the pattern you plan.

The solution is to tie your treadles so that the following happens:

Treadle 1 activating harnesses 12
Treadle 2 activating harnesses 23
Treadle 1 activating harnesses 12
Treadle 6 activating harnesses 34
Treadle 5 activating harnesses 14
Treadle 6 activating harnesses 34

With the mastery of this principle, you can retie those treadles with speed and assurance to any treadling pattern in any book—or to a pattern in your head for that matter.

There are several advantages if you hold a boat shuttle like this as you shoot it and strive to catch it in exactly the same position. The main one is that the index finger gives an involuntary push, which is a nice head start to the journey. And your fingers won't get in the way of the weft as it unreels through the slot in the front of the shuttle.

Learn to catch the shuttle with your second hand in the same position as your first hand threw it. In addition to the advantages mentioned in the previous caption, your thumb will be where it belongs—on top of the bobbin—which will prevent the bobbin from spinning at the end of the trip across the warp. Now the shuttle is ready to throw back again. That means no juggling to get it ready, and therefore no interruption in the rhythm. These are good points to remember, and I think you will see their value the more you weave.

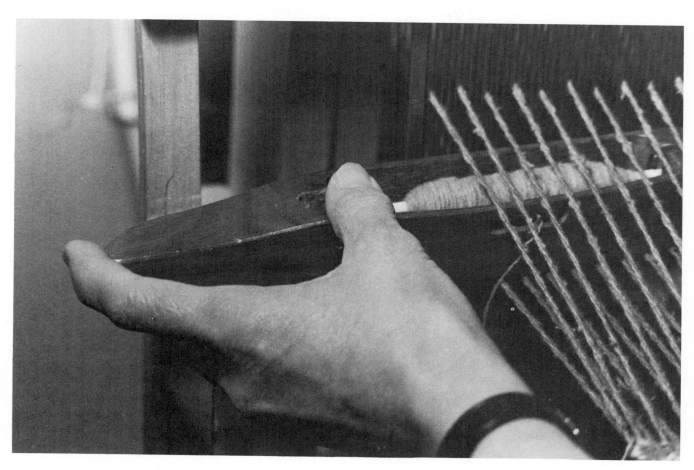

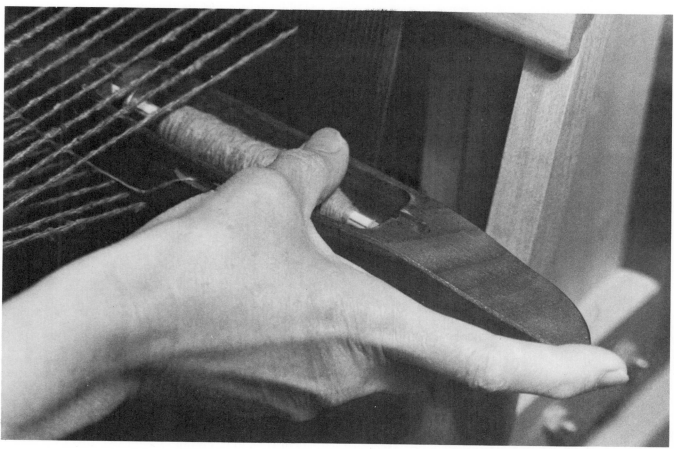

A Uniform Beat Is Important

In any project from wall hangings to yard goods, the beat is extremely important. If you weave a yard on Tuesday when you are cross with the world, and weave a yard on Wednesday when life seems wonderful, there may be a great difference in the density of the fabric. Strive for uniformity of beat, if not of temper.

Unweaving After You Have Slammed the Beater. If by mistake you should really slam the beater, you must take out a few picks, that is, unweave back to the point where the density is uniform. No, the heavily beaten part will not come out in the cleaning or the washing—absolutely not—I've tried it.

A Sample Warp On a Wide Loom—the Beat Is Even More Important. If you are making a narrow sample on a wide loom, this matter of beat is even more important. You can certainly see that a 40" (124.5 cm) beater's force against a 2" (5.1 cm) wide sample is going to be much greater than the same 40" (124.5 cm) beater's force against even a 26" (66 cm) wide warp.

If you make the 2" (5.1 cm) sample and then the 26" (66 cm) wide warp, you must work for the same number of picks per inch on each piece. This will require an extremely light beat on the 2" (5.1 cm) sample, and a heavy one on the 26" (66 cm) piece. On different projects there will be enough variations to provide an endless supply of bookmarks and ironing bags.

What Is Going On Here Is . . .

While you are actually weaving, it is good to remember what you are doing with that warp and weft.

You are not laying a pick of weft flat and straight from selvedge to selvedge, although it seems you are. You are laying that weft *over* some warp ends and then *under* some others.

Selvedge to Selvedge Equals More Than Warp Width. With this in mind, it will probably make more sense that all the weaving books, including this one, suggest you lay the weft into the shed at an angle, or an arc, or in scallops for unusually heavy wefts. You need more than a 26" (66 cm) weft to get across the 26" (66 cm) warp we discussed a few paragraphs before. If the weft is very heavy, you might need 30" (76.2 cm).

You need enough length to go from selvedge to selvedge, but without drawing in at the sides as you beat. The warp should be the same width after the beat as it is with the shed open. Keep that in mind and you should be safe.

Warp Take-Up Occurs Too. As for the warp, remember it too does not just lie there. If the weft goes over and under the warp, then just as surely the warp goes under and over the weft. From this we can easily deduce there will be warp length lost by take-up in the warp as the weaving progresses.

How Much You Have Woven and How to Check

There are all sorts of tricks for measuring the length of what you have woven. But I still think the simplest is—with the tension off—to measure with a tape measure, then to make some sort of note somewhere (perhaps on your treadling direction sheet), and to stick a huge safety pin into the weaving at that point.

Another satisfactory method is the Collingwood method by which you make a tie at one selvedge every foot, do it again after the next foot, and then put a different color to mark the end of a yard.

I must admit that one time I did an extra yard because the purple tie got folded back into the warp somehow. Some people are not at all clever, and I do not mean Mr. Collingwood.

Playing with the Last Part of the Warp
If you know you have figured generously, are positive you have woven enough for the project with an allowance for shrinkage in the finishing, and are lucky enough to have extra warp left, then you can be in for some fun.

Variations Possible. Whatever half filled bobbins you have around, or crazy treadling you have in mind (perhaps some ricrac you have always wanted to try as weft, or some ribbon?) all these have a place on your "free" warp.

An Ancient Variation Is Possible Too. You could even try out the overshot weave, although the chances are your warp won't be threaded to it.

On a four-harness loom you can get four different blocks—one for every pair of harnesses except the two tabbies. They will be the 12 block, the 23 block, the 34 block, and the 14 block. If your threading is 1 2 1 2 1 2 1 2 3 4 1 4 when you treadle the 12 on a sinking shed loom, the first eight threads on the left will fall, as well as the end threaded on harness 1 between the two 4's. You can see you will get quite an overshot (where the weft *shoots* over the warp).

The directions for overshot usually tell you to make a block by treadling 12—or some other pair of harnesses—six times, four times, or whatever the size of block he/she wants.

Of course you cannot treadle 12, put the shuttle through, beat, and treadle 12 again. The weft would not be locked in at all or be placed correctly, and the whole thing would look terrible. What is assumed here is that you will use two shuttles—one will be the warp material and the other a pattern yarn (usually much heavier and of a softer twist).

When the treadling directions say 12 3×, 23 5×, they are telling you in a shortened fashion to do the following:

> 12 pattern yarn
> 13 warp yarn, starting from the left
> 12 pattern yarn
> 24 warp yarn, starting from the right
> 12 pattern yarn
> 13 warp yarn, starting from the left
> 23 pattern yarn
> 24 warp yarn, starting from the right, etc.

The reason for the warp yarn shuttle starting from the left when you are doing 13 tabby and from the right when you are doing 24 tabby is just to get you into a habit. If when you pick up the tabby shuttle at the right selvedge, you KNOW you'll be using 24 tabby, you will have one thing less to worry about.

On a complicated overshot project you will have quite enough to do keeping track of the pattern picks, without worrying about which tabby you should be using. Unfortunately, that does make a difference in the appearance of the finished cloth, so be sure to alternate the tabbies.

If you want to make your own overshot designs on graph paper, there are a couple of points that will make the fun easier and more satisfactory. Always have odd threads by evens, that is, thread 3 4 3 4 1 not 3 4 3 4 2. This is to "preserve the tabby," because if you put a 2 next to a 4, two threads will be affected when you treadle 24.

The next point is not one you must abide by, but it is traditional. You can deviate from it at will, but you can see it is one element that gave unity to the old blue and white coverlets you see in museums. It was called "tromp as writ" by our weaving great-grandmothers. If a threading was 1 2 1 2 3 2 3 4 1 4 1 4 1 4 you started the first block with 14 treadling. You wove that square—enough picks of the 14 treadling with the pattern yarn—and the tabby rows, to make a square block. You then went to the next block on the left, which would be tiny and the 34 block. It would overlap the first 14 block by one thread, the 4.

You would progress to the left again and treadle the 23 block, which would be twice as large as the 34 block because it was composed of twice as many warp threads. The 23 block overlaps the one to its immediate right by one thread again, this time a 3.

And now you get to the 12 block. After you have woven that one square, you will see it too has one thread in common with the previous or 23 block.

Now I hope the rule that says each block should have one thread in common with the previous block makes sense. You may not, by this rule, have a 23 block by a 14 block. You may have a 23 by a 34 or by a 12. You may have a 14 by a 34 or a 12.

Nobody expects you to make a coverlet, but this weave is most useful for new bag straps or bands to be sewn on dark dinner skirts. These projects, unlike the coverlet, would give you a chance to try out the weave and see if you consider it a delight or merely an annoyance.

And Don't Forget That Magic Old Double Weave. Should your warp have been threaded to 1234, you can double weave on your "free warp." This weave is fun, provides substance for group workshops, and can literally bring a third dimension to your weavings.

The basic theory starts from when you realize that the minimum number of harnesses necessary to weave a cloth is two. You have four and can then somehow make double cloth.

Write the numbers 1 through 4 on the fingernails of one hand—the 1 and 3 in one color and the 2 and 4 in a contrasting color. These numbers represent the warp ends. 1 and 3 are for now the top cloth. 2 and 4 are the back cloth—the part you can't see without a mirror or without getting under the loom to look at the underside of the warp.

If you lift harness 1 (sinking shed loom, sink 234) and put a pick of weft in, you have woven one pick on the top cloth. Do all these steps first by raising your marked fingers and it becomes ridiculously clear.

Now you want to weave a pick on the back cloth. Raise *all* the top cloth—all the 1's and all the 3's—plus half of the back cloth, which we shall say is the 2. You now have 123 harnesses *up* (sinking shed loom, sink 4). Put in a pick of weft.

You now have one pick on the top cloth and one pick on the bottom cloth. You want to do the other possible pick on the top cloth, and the other possible pick on the bottom cloth. So far, your treadling would look like this:

Rising Shed	Sinking Shed
1	234
123	4

The opposite pick on the top cloth would be 3, so raise harness 3 (sinking shed loom, sink 124) and put in a pick of weft. What you have done now looks like this:

Rising Shed	Sinking Shed
1	234
123	4
3	124

To get a pick into the back cloth raise all the top cloth plus the opposite half of the back cloth. It would have to be 134 (sinking shed loom, sink 2). Put in a pick of weft. The complete treadling unit for this aspect of the weave is:

Rising Shed	Sinking Shed
1	234
123	4
3	124
134	2

If you will continue this for an inch or more, and then treadle 13 together, you will find that a tube has formed into which you can drop pennies or whatever other little treasures you wish to hide forever. To lock this tube you must reverse the top cloth and the bottom cloth.

What will happen is the unwoven warps from the 13 top cloth will reposition themselves and become the back cloth. Similarly the back cloth warps will come to the surface and be the top cloth.

All this is much easier to see if you have a two color warp, one color on 1 and 3 and the other on 2 and 4. Here again be sure to do it with your marked fingers before you do it on the loom. The new treadling will look like this:

Rising Shed	Sinking Shed
2	134
124	3
4	123
234	1

You can make cloth twice as wide as your loom if you will make "half a tube," that is, have two selvedges to the left or right (top cloth and bottom) selvedge, and what is usually selvedge at the opposite edge becomes a fold.

This requires two shots on the top cloth, and then two shots on the bottom cloth. But you must start your first top pick at the side you have decided is to be the fold, going over to the selvedge. The second top one starts at the selvedge and goes back to the fold. The same goes for the back cloth—start at the fold and go to the selvedge, and come back from the selvedge to the fold. Again four shots equal the total treadling unit for this aspect.

If you use one shuttle of orange and one of yellow, with an orange and yellow alternating warp, you can have an all orange top (or bottom) cloth and an all yellow bottom (or top) cloth. Or you can have an orange warp crossed by yellow weft on the top—or the bottom. And a yellow warp crossed with orange on the bottom—or the top. By not interlocking those yarns at the selvedges you can make two entirely separate cloths. Interlock them at the selvedges and you will have multi-colored tubes, the colors depending on the treadling and the order of the shuttles.

You do not have to change sheds at the selvedges either. You can do it anywhere you choose to. The kitchen wall hanging mentioned in this book—the one with side pockets for wooden spoons—was made on this principle.

When you set up a warp for double weave, remember you are weaving two cloths, one on top of the other. Therefore if the correct sett for the warp yarn is 20, the sett should be 40 for double weave. For a double weave cloth, check the first sample carefully. You may find a lengthwise streak at the fold, even after the cloth has been steam pressed. When you make the next sample, sley looser at the fold side for two or three dents. An example would be that, instead of sleying 3 to a dent, do 2-1-2. If you are single sleying, then skip a dent like this, 1-0-1.

And if you have an uncatching or double catching end at the fold, cut it and take it to the back beam so that it won't interfere with the other ends of the warp.

Now if you can find yourself directions for Finnvav we probably won't see you back here reading for months!

Retie the Treadles for More Freedom. You might want to retie the treadles for this part of the weaving, to the following:

Treadle 1	13
Treadle 2	1
Treadle 3	2
Treadle 4	3
Treadle 5	4
Treadle 6	24

It will give you a lot of freedom. If you want to sink three treadles at once, it is easy—one with one foot and two with the other.

Results You Can Expect, and Some to Surprise You
Sometimes this weaving will give you ideas for the next project. Other times it will solve problems, some of which you never knew you had. And at the very least, you might get some rousing good pot holders or traveling shoe bags.

14.
Buying a Loom

My contention is not that buying a loom is as hard as buying a house, but the law of averages says you will probably have the loom longer. So be warned.

The Types Available

There are really three types of looms in current coin: counter-balanced, jack, and contre-marche. The latter type you will see very seldom. The first you will see too often. The middle one is a joy to own or use.

Counter-Balanced Looms. The counter-balanced loom is the one used in old colonial restorations—with rollers above the harnesses, on which are wrapped cords. The harnesses, those picture frame-like parts, sink when a treadle is depressed. This is why counter-balanced looms are referred to as sinking shed looms. They are made in the United States today; most European looms I have seen are sinking shed.

Jack Looms. Jack looms have a mechanism under the harnesses that either pushes the harnesses up, or works with other parts of the mechanism to pull the harnesses up. This action makes the shed, which is why they are referred to as rising shed looms.

Contre-Marche Looms. Looms of this type are tied both up and down to make sheds. They are a whole subject in themselves. The Handweavers Guild of America has an authority on contre-marche looms and runs a column about them in their quarterly magazine. Write to them if you are interested. They can probably give you sources, too, as well as construction principles. These looms have both advantages and disadvantages.

Sizes They All Come In. Looms come in many sizes, from the little metal table one that has an eight inch weaving width to some that have 16-20 harnesses, and are better than 60" (152 cm) wide. You can see there is a very wide selection.

How to Choose a Loom for You

Your choice should be governed by several factors: 1) Use; 2) need; 3) budget; 4) who you are.

Use is fairly simple. Will you be making coverlets 90" (229 cm) wide, or 5'×12' (1.5 m×3.6 m) wall hangings? If so, an 8" (20.3 cm) loom will leave something to be desired—width for one; and that is only the beginning of your problems.

Need is another important point. Do you need a loom to go through a door so that it can be removed from the living room when you are not weaving? Be sure to get one that folds—at least enough to go through the doorway. And measure the doorway you have in mind!

Is There a Good Weaving Space?

Is there a good weaving space? That is, the space between the beater when it is laid back against the harness-containing assembly (called the castle) and the front beam. Obviously on a small table loom there will be less space than on a large floor loom. This again, like a lot of things in life, is a matter of relativity.

The Height of a Loom Is Important

Are you taller than average? Sit at the loom before you buy it if you possibly can. Don't neglect this step because you may wind up trying to sell it before there is a scratch on it. Or you may learn to loathe weaving because it gives you a backache.

When you sit at a loom, you should not feel as though you are trying out doll furniture. Conversely you should not have to use the treadles with your toes because that is the only part of your foot that will reach the treadles.

Sitting at a loom should be as comfortable as sitting in a comfortable chair at the appropriate table height. If it is not, then there should be no purchase made. And, remember, height of the weaver is not the final answer. Some people are short waisted and some are long waisted. Given the same height of these two people, with one being long waisted and one short waisted—obviously one is going to have longer legs. And longer legs reach farther, whether we are talking about length of walking stride or to treadles under a loom.

The beater should be at a reasonable height so that reaching to beat will be easy and natural. The old rule was, I believe, when you are seated at the loom there should be a right angle between your forearm resting on the breast beam and your body, sitting up straight. As with a lot of the old rules, this one works out well in practice.

Other Questions to Ask

Are the treadles easy to retie? More and more different methods are available to retie treadles. Some are the old loop and snitch cords, chains, pins with bent ends, a single cleverly knotted cord, a loop caught with a pin running through screw eyes on the treadle—and probably more than these by now.

Look over this aspect of any loom you are considering, because if you get something you do not like, or cannot retie easily, you are in for long-term irritation.

If the loom is to go in the living room will it fit, or will it look out of place?

The length of the space behind the castle to the back beam is important too because on that length depends—partly—the size of your shed.

To repeat, the shed is the space between the layers of thread, made when the loom is being woven on and a treadle is depressed. And it is through that space you put your shuttle.

Various Kinds of Heddles Are Important

String heddles or metal? And, if metal, flat heddles or wire? This question will doubtless be coming up more often as we get more Northern European looms in America.

The string heddle appears to be a Scandinavian tradition. They are not going to change, and why should they? They would have to radically change the designs of their looms to do so.

I never could see the advantage of string heddles at all, until an old old weaver told me they were so nice and quiet she could weave while talking on the telephone. If that is your bent, by all means get string heddles.

There is another, more serious, advantage to string heddles that does not occur to a lot of people. Supposing in your warp you are using yarns that are either going to wear and fuzz as they are eased through the heddles when advancing the warp, or have lumps and slubs that are going to stick in the heddle eyes as you try to ease them through. String heddles with their huge eyes are the only convenient answer I know.

Before you tie some to put on your loom, let us stop and think a minute. Remember we said before that if you have a sinking shed loom the top of the string heddle eye must be at the same height as the top of the eye of the neighboring metal one? And that if you have a rising shed loom, the bottom of the heddle eye must be at precisely the same point as the bottom of the neighboring metal one? The reason is that, on a sinking shed loom, the bottom half of the shed is made at the point where the heddles are sunk, and is defined by the top limit of the heddle eye.

Naturally the reverse holds true for rising shed looms. Remember this principle and you can put string heddles on where you wish, using them in conjunction with metal heddles with no trouble at all.

If your loom comes with string heddles and you wish to use metal ones, it is more complicated. You cannot just remove the strings and put on metals—not on the looms I have seen. When string heddles are used, in most cases, the loom has no harness frames as we know them (the picture frame devices with additional rods or bars fitted at top and bottom, on which the heddles slide across back and forth). String heddles appear on looms with "heddle bars" and that is just what they are, top and bottom bars onto which the heddles are slid. Tension is maintained by attaching the top bar to the overhead assembly with the previously mentioned cords, and the bottom bar to the treadle and lamm assembly, again with cords.

Another point, don't think you can just tie metal heddles onto heddle bars and all will be well. If you tie them evenly and tightly enough so they won't hop off the bar ends, you will have trouble sliding them readily as you thread. If you insist on that procedure, or are forced into it by circumstances, then run a strong thread through the bottoms of all metal heddles you have tied on. And knot it.

Or you might figure out how to attach thin metal bars to the heddle bars and put the metal heddles on them in a way that will permit them to slide easily—and have the eyes where they should be. Whatever you do at the bottoms of the heddles, do the same at the tops. It won't be perfect, but it may help.

The Great Floor Loom vs Table Loom Controversy

Now we get to the great floor loom versus table loom controversy.

If you have space problems, the answer seems to be a table loom. When you think about it, the answer is not quite so easy. On what table will you put this loom? The table must be a good height for at least one chair in your domicile—or one chair plus a book or two. And that table must be a strong one to start with, or it will be a rickety one in a woefully short time. It does not have to be heavy at all; I use an antique pine kitchen table when I am using a table loom. But it must be tight and sturdy to withstand the constant clang of harnesses as they rise or drop to make a shed or return to neutral position.

If you have a budget problem and it is either no loom or a table loom, there is no contest—take the table loom and start weaving. Table looms are also good to start children weaving. I am speaking here of the very cheap two-harness looms as well as the more sophisticated four- and eight-harness looms that are far too expensive to be in the toy category.

The one drawback I find in the little wooden two-harness looms we all see at the Christmas toy counters is that nobody tells you what to do after you finish the warp that is already on it. We discuss this later on in this book. I have now decided they were really intended for Scandinavian children whose mothers have warping frames or mills that are as much an integral part of the house as six-slice toasters are in ours.

I still don't understand why they can't drill holes in the bottom of that strong little frame, and supply you with removable dowels to make a temporary warping frame, and give you the directions for making a warp. Either I don't frequent the right toy stores, or I am ahead of my time.

Various Types of Metal Heddles

With many detours, which were really more amplifications than detours, we are on the subject of metal heddles. They come in two basic types: flat steel and wire.

Flat steel are prettier, more stylish, and absolutely frustrating to put on the harnesses if they are not tied in proper order on thread or wire while they are off the harnesses. *TIE AT THE TOPS AND AT THE BOTTOMS* if you value your sanity. They press together better, giving you more heddles to the inch without tangling, than wire heddles. But note—with a magnifying glass if necessary—how they are arranged (left to right and top to bottom) on the loom and keep to that arrangement. If you are right-handed and try to thread them when the previous loom user was left-handed, it will be almost impossible.

The harnesses must be flipped over, bottom to top, to make threading feasible. This makes the eyes enterable from the right, not the left. Flat steel heddles are easier to thread, under many conditions, than any others. But they do have smaller eyes than wire heddles, which can be a distinct disadvantage when using some of the heavier, fuzzier warp yarns.

Some looms do not have harnesses that may be turned over, bottom to top. In this case, shove all the heddles to the center of a harness, tie together with string, take the harness out of the loom, lay it on the floor, and remove the heddle bars from the harness itself very carefully. Reverse the heddle bars, top to bottom, so that the back is the front and the front is the back—just flip them as you would a pancake—and reposition them in the harness. Then put the harness back into the loom and repeat the process for the rest of the harnesses.

The old-fashioned wire heddles tangle more—look carefully at a wire heddle and you will see the reason. But they do come with different sized eyes. I had heard about, and recently found, a type of heddle with huge eyes for the heavy yarns we all become enamored of. They are marvelous; seek them out—they are truly worth it. Wire heddles, like the string heddles, have no "real" right or left to them. They are also cheaper than flat steel.

Metal vs Wooden Harness Frames

Metal harness frames versus wooden harness frames could be a great conversational starter too. Logic dictates that wooden frames could be a liability in damp climates. They could be expected to warp or stick in their wooden tracks, and could give problems whenever the barometer falls.

But I know a wonderful loom maker who lives on Cape Cod. He makes wooden harnesses. I have a friend who lives in Bermuda—and her looms have wooden harnesses. No problems in either case—so much for logic.

Metal frames do have an advantage over wooden ones. In a smaller space you can get more harnesses because metal of a given strength is thinner than its equivalent in wood. If you want a multi-harness loom, it might make a difference to you—if you have a short reach. You can surely buy a loom with twelve or sixteen wooden harnesses that has been properly engineered to give you a clean shed. That is, the back harnesses are higher in a multi-harness sinking shed loom, and the back harnesses are lower in a rising shed loom. But if your reach is exceptionally short, it won't be much fun to thread.

The "Looks" of the Various Looms

Looks are really a matter of taste, but it is necessary to discuss their importance. If this loom is to go in your living room, how do you want it to appear—traditional, functional, light wood or dark? Do you want it as a definite part of the living room, or something to be brought out occasionally and used now and then? Think about these questions as long as you would think about a new couch, and you should make the right decision.

A second-hand loom versus a new one could be another good topic for long conversations, but it becomes less and less of a topic, as back orders for looms pile up. One of the best looms on the market has a thirty-month waiting list. Another exceptionally good loom has a two-year waiting period. I have used both. I consider one much more desirable for my needs, though each is very good looking. Write to the loom manufacturers for literature on the looms you think you might want; enclose a stamped self-addressed envelope, and peruse at your leisure.

If you find a loom at a tag sale and you can find a weaver to go with you, consider it seriously if the person recommends it. Probably you won't be so lucky. I was, but that was about fifteen years ago and a lot of people have taken up the hobby since, as you may have noticed.

Prices Today

The prices you can expect to pay (today as this is being written, not the date it will be published) for a loom range from about $60.00 for the little metal one, to over $1,000.00 for a ten-harness model with better than 50" (127 cm) weaving width. An average price would be $400.00 for a four-harness 30-36" (76.2 cm-91.4 cm) width. Again, I emphasize, I am quoting *today's* prices.

A good little floor loom 20" (51 cm) weaving width is available—at just over $200.00—but again there is a waiting list. And it isn't the stoutest loom I've ever seen.

When you send for the loom literature, ask for the waiting time figure for *all* models from each maker. This might make a difference in your decision.

Where to Rent a Loom
If you belong to a guild, try to rent the kind of loom you think you might like. Take it home, weave on it, get to know its crotchets as it will get to know yours, and find out if you are compatible.

Now that you know some of the questions to ask the seller—and yourself—write down your questions for the seller before you write the letter or make the visit to him.

There is always the possibility you might find *THE LOOM* for you, either new or secondhand. You wanted metal frames, but this has wood; you wanted pin tie-up, but this has cords . . . . But this is your loom, you know it, the price is right, and it is comfortable to sit at. How can I argue with you? Get it and enjoy it.

Direct Tie-Up Looms
Some four-harness looms have only four treadles, as we discussed a while ago. This does not mean the maker scrimped, or the previous owner wore out two treadles. This is known as the direct tie-up. When you press down one treadle, you raise one harness only. There is no way you can change this, it is a built-in feature. However, for many purposes it is very handy. These are usually rising shed looms, but I have seen one that operates on the sinking shed principle.

If you want to see what you can do with a given threading, which means a lot of different treadlings, you are saved the bother of retying treadles. If your directions say to depress three of the four harnesses, put one foot on two treadles and the other foot on the third required treadle simultaneously. Very easy.

Many people achieve the same thing on a six-treadle loom by tying the middle four treadles to one harness each, while hunting the treadling they want for a project.

Some Notes On the Use of the Word Treadling
Treadling is the term always used for raising/lowering harnesses to gain a certain effect with a certain threading. If you have a table loom and you lift or lower levers to make a shed, this is still called treadling, which is a difficult concept to some people. To summarize, on a floor loom you treadle with your feet; on a table loom you treadle with your hands. If you can understand this, no other weaving concept, ever, should give you much trouble.

Buying a Loom Bench
Buying a loom bench is not as complicated as buying a loom. Though it is not as easy as buying a chair. You might say it is like buying a chair—with a few other considerations.

First, is it comfortable for you? If it fails this test don't buy it, even if it is made to go with the loom you have decided to buy. The angle of the seat may be wrong. Yes, some benches are made with a slope toward the loom from the back of the bench. I know one ingenious bench and loom maker who has engineered his bench so the angle is capable of change with the adjustment of a couple of screws.

There is also the matter of accessibility. If the seat top covers the whole bench, how will you get at your new bobbins to replace those used up as you weave? Where will you keep scissors, tape measures, other shuttles, etc? Of course, having a table right beside your loom means the accessibility factor is quite irrelevant. But few living room looms, in my experience, have that luxury.

Swedish Loom Baskets

There is an imaginative Scandinavian answer to the shuttles and bobbins problem, but it appears to work only for the looms that are bigger and of heavier construction than ours, with overslung beaters. It is a basket, with formed handles, to hook over a side member of the loom. No space for this exists on most looms I know. However, if you get one for a present, be grateful; it is still a handy thing to have.

Pockets Must Be Neat

Do you really want open pocket-like boxes at either end of your loom bench? They do hold a lot that you will be needing; but if they aren't kept neat, they will only add to the clutter of a living room. A mug of tea can be comfortably at hand in an end pocket though, with no problem of tipping it over, because most of it is below the pocket rim.

What to Do If It Is Not Quite Right

If the bench you really want is too high by an inch or so, do get a carpenter to cut off the legs because I have yet to see the amateur who can get all four legs even. You are sure to end up with a three-legged bench with one wiggly leg.

Refinish the bench to match your loom if it is in the living room. If it is in another room, follow your inclinations as to whether or not you should refinish it. A wonderful amount of weaving can be done in the time it takes to refinish a bench! And life is short, even when you are very young.

The best loom bench I ever had, from a sheer comfort point of view, was a dreadfully tired old kitchen stool painted an equally dreadful red, and held together with baling wire. It was precisely the right height for the loom it was used with, and the wide rungs were at the exact place to easily hook your heel between treadlings. The loom it went with had no front cross-bar to put your foot on, and the treadles were hung at the back, so you could not rest a foot on one, without considerably changing the resultant pattern.

Of the Ideal Bench and Adjusting to Reality

The loom bench I would like to see does not, to the best of my knowledge, exist. It would have a box under the seat with a deep drawer as well. It would also have a shelf under the seat that would pull out when you needed it and disappear when you did not.

The preceding paragraphs were intended to make you understand that a bench is part of the weaving equipment. As with any equipment, it doesn't matter how expensive or beautifully designed it is. The important factor is, does it fit your needs and solve the majority of your problems?

Remember my old red stool and use your judgment.

15.
Books, Periodicals, and Monographs

Books are nice. Books are helpful. Books are necessary. This applies to weavers as well as to the rest of the world.

But it is a fact of life that most weaving books are expensive, and likely to get more so. If you have any sort of budget limitation, you might make yourself a five-year plan for books that you 1) need; 2) want; and 3) don't need but do want.

Books You Will Need

The absolute minimum of weaving books, aside from this one, I would guess are: *A Handweaver's Pattern Book* by Marguerite P. Davison, and *New Key To Weaving* by Mary E. Black.

Books You Will Want

You will eventually want to own these two marvels: *The Techniques of Rug Weaving* by Peter Collingwood and *Designing and Drafting for Handweavers* by Berta Frey.

The Berta Frey book is still in print, and hopefully it will remain so forever. I cannot imagine a substitute for this; but there may be—or one might be forthcoming.

With the book you are reading and the above-mentioned Davison book, you can warp a loom and have patterns to weave forever. Add Black and Collingwood and you will have ideas for at least the same length of time.

When you open the Collingwood book, think of a cookbook. You do not have to make a croquembouche daily. Somewhere in most cookbooks you can learn to boil an egg. So it is with the Collingwood weaving book, which has very simple and beautiful ideas.

Books You Will Want, but Not Need

If you think that books are to expand your horizons, see what has been done, see what is being done, and see what could be done, then you will have to make a safari to a craft book store.

I will warn you of the temptations there—beautiful books, useful books, big books, small books, monographs, magazines, all sorts of money-gobbling items. There is only one way to come out with the rent money intact. Before you go in decide how much you are going to spend—and stick to your decision. Ask them to lay a book aside for you until payday—I feel that is playing the game, but don't buy or charge it.

Guild Libraries as a Source

Join a weaver's guild as soon as you can for many reasons. Most guilds have libraries, and you may borrow books you think you might want before you purchase them. Weaving books are not like novels; you want to own them whether you ever read them or not. The value of weaving books is not in the first reading; it is in the second, or the tenth re-reading on a subject or of a chapter.

Why Read What You Are Not Interested In?

At the start of your weaving career, try to read books on the general subject, not specific aspects of it. If you know you will never weave a wall hanging, quickly read those chapters. Even if you loathe blue and white coverlets, skim the paragraphs on these. This broad emphasis is not designed to make you an all-round expert, but is to make you at least familiar with all aspects of the craft. It is also because once the word gets out in your neighborhood that you weave, you will get questions you simply would not believe.

I spin—a little—but have a low wheel not a wool wheel. Believe me, the differences in operation are considerable. Recently a man who had just bought a nearby restaurant called The Spinning Wheel phoned to say he had what he thought was a spinning wheel. But he said it didn't look anything like the spinning wheel on the menu—and, please, what was it. He was inordinately pleased when I told him that he had a perfectly legal honest to goodness antique wool wheel.

Now for another example. When your friend's son brings a heavy bed cover he had woven in New Zealand, which he tried to finish the night before he left—but doesn't know how to finish or cut in half to sew together—you won't want to say, "Me, I'm a wall hanging person, I just don't know."

Read everything you can on all aspects of the craft. Make a place mat or two from one of the borrowed books. Try a wall hanging, perhaps a little like the one you saw in a book. Try it all out; the books will keep you from getting into a rut.

Periodicals, What They Are and How to Get Them

Now for the magazines and periodicals. You'll need these things urgently, particularly if you live in a rural area with no yarn or book stores.

Currently only one American weaving magazine is printed on a regular basis: *Shuttle, Spindle & Dyepot*, published by The Handweavers Guild of America, Inc., 65 La Salle Road P.O. Box 7-374, West Hartford, Connecticut 06107. It is the quarterly house organ of HGA and a great magazine. A few years ago it was a great *little* magazine, but it is now so good, knowledgeable, helpful, and beautiful that it has grown well out of the *little* category. If you have questions, they will answer; they have a whole column devoted to Q & A's. If the editor cannot answer your question, it is not buried, but given out to the membership for help. So do join HGA and read every word in *SS&D*.

There was another magazine, a strictly commercial venture, called *Handweaver & Craftsman*. Sometimes the ten- or twenty-year-old issues appear for sale—buy them because they are very useful.

Several yarn suppliers publish little folders, booklets, or brochures. They have yarn news and usually a pattern with a real sample attached. You must pay for these, but why not? Would you send letters full of handy information to people you have never met, on a regular basis, with the postal rates what they are? Write, enclosing a self-addressed, stamped envelope, asking for current subscription prices on these: *Warp and Weft*, Robin & Russ, 533 N. Adams St., McMinnville, Oregon 97128, and *Looming Arts*, Mary Pendleton, Jordan Road, Sedona, Arizona 86336.

Advantages of Monographs

When you are in the bookstore, or at the guild library table, you must be sure not to miss the slim slender items that look like file folders, with either printed or typed covers. These are usually monographs, and they are very useful.

If you did not understand the description of a given weaving process in one book, you might well catch it with another person's point of view. And if you only wanted an $8.00 book because it gave a description of Finnvav, wouldn't it be better to find it in a $4.00 monograph that really concentrates on the subject?

16.

Keeping Records, Notebooks, and Yarn Samples

This is a most important part of weaving if you are at all limited on time. And everyone I know is.

Why You Should Keep Records
Records do not have to be kept in a preordained form, but they should be in a consistent form. Notes you make this year should be understandable five years from now.

One of the easiest record forms to use is the pad of sheets that The Handweavers Guild of Connecticut sells for the benefit of their scholarship fund. There is a place for date, pattern, technique, source, purpose, threading, tie-up, treadling, warp, weft, reed, sett, sley, width in reed, weft shots per inch, and notes on the results. Ten years from now I believe you will be glad you read this paragraph!

How to Keep Records and Be Efficient About It
An absolute minimum, if you don't choose to buy those marvelously handy 8½"×11" (22 cm × 28 cm) pads, is:

Warp—width and length, with sample attached

Weft—with sample attached

Reed size—with sett and sley

Threading

Tie-up

Treadling

Date

Source of pattern

Also attach a sample of the finished weave if you can manage it. Otherwise a piece of the sample warp you surely did before the project warp.

The most important part of the record is your comments. Did it do what you wanted? Was the "hand" what you had in mind? Did the colors give the effect you wanted? What particular problems did you encounter—sticky warp, difficulty in maintaining an even beat, hard time rolling on at an even tension? What did you learn from this warp? How would you use the same warp again differently?

Notebooks—What and Why

An 8½"×11" (22 cm × 28 cm) notebook that is labeled with dates on the cover is handy, quick, and easy to refer to.

Please keep your records as you go along. The time given to do this is only a few minutes, and the grief it saves is so much. It is vital, even if you are not a record-keeping type of person.

Examples of Useful Information. If your best friend raves about a blue scarf you made, but you know she prefers gray, all you have to do is refer to the notes, buy the thread in gray instead of blue, wind the warp, count heddles, thread, sley, tie on, and weave it off. It should take two evenings if you go to bed at a reasonable hour, three at the most.

And there will be no wracking your brain to remember if the yarn was light sports weight, or that heavy baby weight you tried out. There is a sample of it attached to the record sheet.

No searching the mind for the pattern, and then sitting down with graph paper to plot out the threading. It is right on the record sheet. And there is also a recommendation on the record sheet to use hair spray on this warp to keep it from being so sticky; and to depress the treadles one at a time to the often required three, which seemed to make the threads less sticky.

Oh, yes, it all comes back to you now, that terrible warp. But it was lovely. And because you have kept your records well, you won't have to repeat your problems or errors. Once was really enough, now wasn't it?

There, have I convinced you to keep records? For your sake, I do hope so.

How to Organize One. Frankly my notebook is a mess. It is a beautiful big three-hole binder, for which my daughter even made an embroidered cover. It is a total disaster when anyone tries to find something in it—except me. And in case you are wondering why the confession, it was all for the last two words of the preceding sentence, *except me*. I can find anything I want in that notebook in not more than five minutes at the most; and the five minutes includes looking at something I had forgotten or didn't remember I had.

This is to show you we all keep different types of notebooks. I take notes in whatever workshops or seminars I attend, and then type them over on notebook paper and put them into the book. What I do not type is, well, let's take a look at a representative selection.

A recipe for a Christmas tree skirt from that great Libby Crawford workshop. Here is the recipe for spinning oil from the Allen Fannin workshop; but I gave my copy of the recipe to a friend who lost it, and I got it again over the phone from another friend. This is why it is in shorthand on a telephone message sheet. On the back of a blue notice that says The Book Barn bookstore has moved are directions for bead leno. My excuse here was that I wanted the new Book Barn address, which is PO Box 256, Avon, Connecticut 06001 (and they are great, helpful, cheery, knowledgeable folk), as well as the directions for the bead leno. So when I cleaned out my bag that night I just chucked the blue slip into the notebook.

In case you need to know, Nell Znamierowski says that ten to twelve pounds of wool will make a 5'×4' (1.5 m × 1.2 m) wool rya rug, which is in the notebook too, gleaned from a workshop with her, doubtless. (And don't miss one of her workshops if she comes even remotely close to your neighborhood.)

There is also a note that Maria Mundal, that weaver of wonderful tapestries, says the King Arthur face in the tapestry at New York's Cloisters is the most impressive example of hatching she knows. I thought of that and her when I saw it again a while back. We never can be sure which of our statements will stay in people's minds, now can we? So a notebook should be many things to many people, but primarily it should work for the owner.

It could be broken up by sections, workshops, seminars, random notes, things you picked up from a borrowed book or pamphlet. Or it could be done by projects, or weaves, or purposes. Or it could be a strictly chronological record. All you have to remember is what year you put something in, on the topic you are currently interested in.

A Notebook Is an Expensive Book. If this seems a casual approach to keeping a notebook, it is. What is not casual at all is my firm belief in the value of a notebook. If a week's workshop costs $50.00, and you have notes from six you have taken at various places and times, you now have a $300.00 book. Even though you may not be a rare book collector, this is a truly valuable item.

Try to find a notebook with a pocket in it to put the uncopied notes into, so they don't get lost between workshop and binder rings. And punch some graph paper to fit into a section—it comes in very handy. We can all write a draft, tie-up, and treadling on the typewriter, but even IBM's wizards can't do a drawdown with multi-colored warp and several wefts with much ease; so keep right on buying that graph paper.

And start your own notebook now, today, pronto. Then keep it up to date.

Yarn Samples—Why Have Them?

If you don't happen to have a thousand dollar inventory of various types of threads, yarn samples are marvelous space and money-saving devices.

If you never use cottons at all, but a casual friend says "use a linen singles that's about a 20/2 cotton size" it will be quicker to find the right size linen in your storage area if you take with you a sample of 20/2 cotton.

Getting Yarn Samples. Yarn samples are procurable by various means, most of which involve a small bit of money. Some places say to send a dollar or so; some want a set of stamped, self-addressed envelopes for monthly or quarterly mailings, and some just send and send and send, once you are on their mailing list.

If we look at the sending of samples from the yarn suppliers' point of view, it is an expensive advertising device for which there is, at least in the smaller houses, no budgetary allocation. This means the owner, in his/her "spare time," cuts the samples.

The reason I am mentioning this is let's be kind to our yarn supplier friends.

What Samples to Get. If you know you will never weave with linen, don't send money and/or envelopes to all linen suppliers. One will do to get the sizes you need. In spite of the dollar or half dollar charge, sending yarn samples still costs them more than that in time spent. They hope to get this back by your future orders. If there are to be no future orders, keep the linen samples supply to the minimum.

If you happen to want linen samples, try to get all the samples you can. The colors and qualities are so different you can drive yourself frantic combining bright samples on a dull day. Does this smooth blue look better with the rough green, or does the rough blue look better with the smooth green? Should they both be rough, so that there is only the play of color? Should they both be smooth so the heavy glaze of those handthrown plates will be accentuated? The only answer, naturally, is to purchase a very small quantity of each with which to sample.

By the time you have looked your samples over thoroughly—and over again more thoroughly—you will know roughly who specializes in what. I suppose samples could be filed tidily by supplier, then sub-filed by type of yarn; but what happens if one supplier has cotton, linen, and acrylics in one mailing on one sheet?

The easiest way, to my thinking, is filing by supplier, with the latest offering on the top of the folder. They do not always put dates on samples, so I put the date of receipt on each card or sheet sent me. This way I won't get my heart set on a project to be made with yarns bought from a man who sells ends of runs only from samples he sent me five years ago.

If you are doing little projects for friends—and believe me you will—a good set of samples is invaluable. For instance, there is the interior decorator grandmother who wants a rug to match wallpaper in the granddaughter's dollhouse. You had better have the numbered samples straightened out for that lady.

A Specific Simple Filing Method for Samples. You will want a red file folder envelope, the sort with ties, for each supplier.

You will write on the outside of each one the supplier's name, and file his offerings in that envelope. Occasionally they do go out of business; but don't throw away the samples, unless you have duplicates of the sizes from other suppliers.

This subject file shouldn't take up more than about six inches (15.2 cm) on any bookshelf, so it isn't a major space investment.

What Samples to Keep and What to Throw Away and When. If you have "odd" suppliers—people who send out samples of stuff that they, or you, class as novelties, giving no size, no type of spin, no useful information—keep them as long as you think they are handy, and throw them out when it seems wise. You don't want to be inundated with paper and samples. In spite of being a weaver, you want space left on your shelves for books on other subjects.

Remember that paper and paperwork in weaving are not ends in themselves. They are useful only as long as they make the weaving easier or more fun, or add to the excitement. We are not trying to make file clerks out of you new weavers. Whatever is simplest for you, and works best to find what you want when you want it—that is the type of system I am attempting to have you establish for yourself.

How to Really Use Samples—and When. Samples should be pulled out and spread around you every so often—when you think it's time to replenish the supply cupboard, and the rent has been paid.

Remember when you order the Scandinavian threads from their country of origin it all takes time. Don't fall in love with a red Swedish linen, or a deep dark Norwegian blue, for a Christmas present—in November.

Christmas starts very early for weavers. If you send for the yarns in August, they arrive the end of September, and your sample is off a little loom by some time in October. There is now only a bit over a month left for weaving before you want to be pressing the finished article and rustling the tissue paper for wrapping and packing.

Check the Stock in Your Friends' Studios Because . . .

When you go to your friends' studios, look about to see what types of threads they buy. Having your own mental inventory can occasionally stand you in a very good stead.

Once upon a time, I didn't know what to get a friend for Christmas. In December she said she wanted a red linen Christmas runner to go over her damask cloth. I remembered the spool of fine Swedish red linen I had seen in a friend's weaving studio, called her, and yes, she still had it, and her red project was finished so this was extra. She hooted at the idea of making sample and runner by Christmas Eve. She was also worried about the quantity she had left. "And there is no more of that dye lot in the States," she said. "I got it from a little place in the mountains four years ago when I was in Sweden."

I gulped when I saw the small amount on the spool. I made a sample to see how the pattern looked with the particular sley and threading I wanted to use. The sample was 12" (30.5 cm) long and 1" (2.5 cm) wide—successful too. I'd put it on a table loom, so if I had been forced to I could have woven about 4" (10.2 cm) total. I did weave 2½" (6.4 cm), and then made the runner warp out of a little more than half of what was left. Warp that is tied onto the front and back can't be woven, but must be wound so warp in this case (or in any other) was more than half the total.

A heavy weft used with a much lighter warp will certainly throw that theory out the window, but here my warp and weft were the same stuff. My math must have been better than I thought it was because I ended up with one runner, one sample, and half a small bobbin of red left over. Sometimes you are just lucky.

All of which has really nothing to do with yarn samples, but may help you to solve a problem one day, so I mention it.

17.
Workshops, Ratings, and Other Weavers

Workshops are not cause for hysterics. Nor are they cause for withdrawing into your shell and saying, "No, no, I'm not advanced enough." If you have the money, the inclination, and the time, then sign up and go. Phrased a little differently, the same philosophy should go for ratings and other weavers.

What You Need to Enjoy a Workshop
Most weavers of my acquaintance have made their own discoveries in the area of workshops, ratings, and other weavers. On the theory that none of us will live to be 200, I believe a few words of encouragement, caution, and experience on these subjects are very much in order, though not included in the weaving books I know.

If you can make a warp, beam it, thread, sley, tie-on, and read a draft, you can get your money's worth from a workshop.

What a Workshop Really Is
Many guilds have workshops on a regular basis. Mine, the Handweavers Guild of Connecticut, has several a year, and the range of subjects is as wide as you could want. The subjects have been exploring color, spinning, Christmas items, double weave, rug weaves, tapestry, embroidery weaves, dyeing, and even more.

An expert is paid by the guild for the day (or two or three days) and you sign up, paying what is usually a ridiculously low fee. A group of eight to fifteen weavers meets for the workshop period.

Should the topic be shadow weave, that is the emphasis and concentration. For the whole period you explore various aspects of shadow weave, find new uses, play with color and textures, learn tricks of that trade, and end up with a little notebook full of ideas that you will try out as soon as you get home.

When you do get home, you will find number one son has come down with chickenpox and the other three never had it, so there will be a certain inevitable time lag between workshop and tryouts. This is a long-winded way of saying make those notes legible, understandable, and not too cryptic.

Some (many, in my experience) workshops have you bringing your own sample loom or folding floor loom. If you don't have one, sometimes you can still get into the workshop because one more financially blessed weaver will bring two or three.

Some workshop leaders will, upon your registration, send the made-up warp to you, complete with threading and sleying directions. This means you do that work before you get to the workshop. A marvelous timesaver because you can start weaving as soon as you get to the studio.

Who Will Go to a Workshop

When you arrive breathless and terrified at your first workshop, you will find weavers there just like you. They will range from about 17 to 83. And the 17-year-old may know more about the technicalities of looms and theories of weaving, to the surprise of many.

It has been a constant source of delight to me, seeing young people mastering and using the intricacies of weaving. Once they realize that they understand what they are doing, and have a good background, they often take off like rockets.

A percentage of the older weavers received a rather haphazard training and, difficult as it may be for the younger generation to believe, the fact is craft centers were not always with us. Thus, some of the older weavers may be superb in only one area that their weaving teacher enjoyed and understood. And some may be accomplished in other areas, but lacking knowledge of something else. For instance, how to level a loom, or how to do some step of weaving efficiently.

As the standards for weaving teachers get higher, I am sure better beginning weavers will be produced. Of course the other side of the coin is that some of the weavers who have been at it for many years are all-around experts because of a natural curiosity. They can do everything and a little more—all done with excellence, assurance, and usually a remarkable modesty.

Workshops are to be enjoyed thoroughly, and don't you let anyone make you forget it. Remember this is a pleasure, not an assignment. You have paid for the privilege, so don't do what you really do not want to do.

The weaver next to you may be an expert, or an absolute novice, a veteran of a one week's beginner course. The real expert may be the vague looking girl in jeans and a batik shirt, and the novice may be the gray-haired grandmother who finally has time to do what she wants with her days.

Don't start putting labels on workshop members because the chances are very good you will have to make up a new set before lunch break.

Ratings Are . . .

There is a wonderful subject to bring up if you like controversy—ratings! Ratings are granted by various guilds, by a ratings board chosen from (usually) master weavers from that guild. Ratings say that, on ascending levels, you have proved to be competent in diverse techniques and with differing sorts of threads. You do a lot of different pieces in different weaves, with different threads, and on different warps—all this in accordance with the directions supplied you. You package up the assortment, send it to the provided address, and chew your nails for a couple of months hoping you will pass.

Points Against Ratings, and Refutations. Since new weavers are always so beautifully enthusiastic about everything to do with weaving, why not start with some of the negative aspects?

People say ratings force you to do what you don't like to do. What good are ratings anyway if you know you are competent, why go to all that bother? Who is to judge? My money is very limited; why buy yarns and weave all that stuff I do not want and will not use? I only have a four-harness loom. I only want to do wall hangings.

Let me tell you that any one of the above sentences is worth a good half day's conversation. All you have to do is find articulate people on each side, and then sit back and listen.

At least in my experience, ratings do not force you to do what you don't want to do. If you want to do only wall hangings, nothing will prevent you doing a wall hanging in a traditional technique—such as crackle weave or summer and winter—and you will learn new techniques you can use to set yourself apart from the majority of wall hanging people.

It is not so easy to refute that why-bother-I-know-I'm competent attitude. But be very sure you know you are. I have a friend who would be mad to spend her time weaving for ratings. She has been weaving and learning for 35 years, winning prizes in juried shows for about that length of time, has written a book, teaches, sells, and is still learning. She is, however, the exception; we must admit that.

Points In Favor of Ratings and Refutations. The other side of the coin is the pro-ratings group.

Weaving for ratings widens the weaving horizons. There is no guilt in weaving for ratings because you know you have to spend the time to try out for the ratings. It is a grand excuse to read the weaving books. And a good way to use up small cones of this and that.

The articulate people on each side of those statements could use up many pots of tea and coffee in discussion.

Refuting the argument that you don't feel guilty about weaving if you know you are doing it for the ratings is a little difficult in some cases. For example, what if you are the mother of small children and can only crank out a scarf or two a year with your free time? Wait a while, madam, before you worry; because you are not getting the most out of your loom anyway. And you will have more free time later, I promise you.

Who YOU Are Should Determine Your Attitude. Ratings, in my opinion, are a spur or a crutch— depending on your point of view. If you are the sort of person who finds a new technique, the reading of books, and the consideration of samples, a completely integral part of weaving, then you may not need ratings. But you may be the one who wants them and wants them very much.

You may look farther and see you are really doing your own ratings. And all people (including weavers) can be harder on themselves than any jury or board.

My position on ratings is identical to the one I hold about snails. If you like them, fine. If you don't, equally fine. But don't say you don't like them until you have tried them—or thought a great deal about trying them.

Weavers Are Individuals, Not Types

If you are a real perfectionist, ratings can get you out of a rut. There are people who will make a table runner, decide after washing and pressing it a dozen times they would prefer to have sleyed at 30epi than 32epi, and then proceed to make one at 30epi. After the washing and pressing routine, they decide they would have preferred the effect of a 10/1 instead of the 20/2—although the size is obviously the same—then they go and do it in the 10/1.

In the Marguerite Davison book on pages viii through x at the beginning of the book, she gives a very short basic explanation of how to figure yardage per pound for yarns of different fibers and different sizes.

Then the table runner lady could decide she would prefer winding together two threads of half the size for the weft, instead of using the double size single. And she could go on and on for years doing the same thing in different colors.

Nobody should quarrel with this as an activity. Each individual is an individual. But have you considered that she may be working in a high pressure office where on every job she handles she wants to spend an hour more to get it right, from her point of view, not that of her boss. Perhaps she has a need for the controlled-to-her-liking type of project. Who really knows what goes on in somebody's head—often including that person?

Other Weavers

Perhaps the following words do not belong in a book on weaving, but rather in one on philosophy. You decide, but I am putting them in now because they might help you in your weaving.

Yes, there are many kinds of weavers, diverse shapes, sizes, and ages—but, concomitantly, they are packaged differently. Should you be inclined to categorize people by looks or clothes, you are in for a high voltage shock with weavers. And very likely a change in your assessment procedures.

I have one weaving acquaintance who looks like somebody's grandmother, the sort who is perennially baking cookies to give to little newsboys when they deliver the afternoon paper. Surprise—she can't cook. But she can, and does, weave multi-harness linen damask napkins your great-great-aunt would have been very proud to own.

There is a gorgeous slim young thing who looks like an absolutely brainless high fashion model. She is the one who turns out impressive vestments for the clergyman in her church . . . and is working for an advanced degree.

What I am urging you when you move to a new town, or even a new state, and appear at your first new guild meeting is not to be too sure that the weaver who looks to be your statistical twin will be your best weaving friend. It might be the very old woman who walks with a cane, received her master's degree over a half century ago, and is quite an authority on art history. Or it might be the casually dressed college girl who is saying to those in her vicinity, "Two simply tremendous things happened last week. I was offered a summer job at Wood's Hole, and I discovered sprang. Oh, and my little brother made Eagle Scout."

As you do not choose your weaving books for their covers, so I urge you not to use that approach with your weaving friends. Like bird-watching and concerts, it just will not work.

Ratings Can Help You If . . .

Stepping for a moment out of the role of objectivity to advocate ratings, I do raise a question. If you propose to do any teaching, it is my experience that the people who do the hiring understand ratings if not weaving.

Suppose two people try out for a weaving job in a crafts center. One says, "I've been weaving twenty years." The other says, "I have my master's rating from Boston Weavers Guild," and takes in their sheet of requirements when she is being interviewed. I could tell you which weaver is the more likely to be hired, but I am sure you can figure it out for yourself—particularly if you have seen the relevant sheet from that guild.

The 20-year veteran may be by far the better weaver, or at the very least a better teacher, but the rating is a form of yardstick for the interviewer. He has probably never heard of the Boston Weavers Guild, but he does know that some authority has said this applicant is knowledgeable. And do not forget the interviewer probably knows nothing of weaving. If he/she did, there would be an excellent chance one of his/her weaving friends would have the job before it was even advertised.

To sum up, ratings are very good for some people at some periods in their lives. Conversely, at some periods in their lives, ratings will be precisely the wrong thing for some people. And in both cases we may be referring to the same people.

Lest you think I am now congratulating myself on having done a successful job of fence straddling, may I add that I honestly do not know how I would vote if this were on a multiple choice ballot.

Weavers Are Problem Solvers, If You Give Them a Chance

At your guild meeting, do bring up any weaving problem you may have. Not just the sticky warp (for which you use spray starch or hair spray on the warp, play the treadles, and start again—hoping). Bring up the where-do-I-get items too. Or the where do I put up a warping frame, in a rented house? One of the great answers to that is take a couple of matched thickness books, put them *under* a row of books on the bookshelves, having them stick out a little, and hang your frame on the resulting great woodworking creation. Or what to do about the skein that is too long for your swift? Take off your shoe, hook one end of the skein over a chair back and the other over your foot, and wind away. Some of these answers I picked up at guild meetings, so heaven only knows what you will come up with.

If you know where you are moving in time to ask at a meeting, "who knows anybody there?" it can be most reassuring, even though you are normally very assured. If you are going off to college, remember they have guilds in college towns too.

Finally if your belief is that most people are basically pretty great, I am sure you will find the same to be true of weavers.

18.
On Being a Good Neighbor

This chapter is not about baking cookies or taking pots of chicken soup to flu-ridden friends, but rather about problems that will arise when people know you weave. The word gets around quickly, so be prepared.

How About Demonstrating In the School?
The first call is likely to come from your neighborhood school. "We hear that you weave, would you like to come and demonstrate for fifty second-graders? At your convenience of course."

Now before you say no, which is probably the normal reaction, ask the school a few questions.

Questions to Ask About Demonstrating. How many in a group? If they don't know, ask for a group of five to ten with about ten minutes devoted to each group. That way you can answer questions from each small person in each group—even the shy members.

Will they have any preparation in the classroom before you meet with them? In other words, will they know a spinning wheel from a loom, or must you explain that to them? Usually the schools will say of course there will be some pre-explanation. Whether they whiz out to write one up, or it is already in the works, is not your problem but strictly theirs.

What to Do and How It Will Be When You Get There. You put a long, coarse, strong warp on your little table loom, and you show up at whatever hour the school asks you—minus a quarter hour.

That gives you a chance to take off your bonnet and shawl, settle yourself down at the angle from which you choose to face the kids, and lay out the items you have brought along for show and tell. When the first group shows up, you can ask them what questions they have as they are watching you weave back and forth. One of the first will be "can I try?"; this is why you have brought along a collection of shuttles with different colors and types of weft on them. A few picks and the next child gets a turn.

You might ask a bored looking boy if he has figured out how the loom works, and tell him that in the colonial days the fathers and brothers made the looms. Or tell another child that tape looms were used in the parlor to weave suspenders, shoulder straps, etc.

And you might dredge up out of your memory any relevant bits of history you can recall. Remind them that fire hoses had to be woven in double weave on a loom before there were fire hose factories. You may not be interested in history, but it is surprising how many of the children are. Don't tell long stories because you won't get a chance to get in the punch line—a new group will arrive, and the previous group will have moved on to watch rug hooking, or candle dipping or whatever.

I feel very strongly that the main thing in these school demonstrations is to permit the children to ask their questions. And if you can't answer one, do be a nice soul and tell the child you will try to find out and let the class know. And do it. Get that child to write down his name, grade, teacher's name, and the question. All this goes into a little notebook you have been provident enough to bring along with you. The school route is not really so terrifying, and the children love it. So why not be a good citizen and say yes? Remember you are something very special in their day.

Loom Queries From Mothers

Another question likely to come up in the middle of January will be asked by a frantic mother, "My aunt/uncle/mother/father gave my son/ daughter a little loom for Christmas, and now he/she has used up all the strings that came on it. What do I do to get some more on?"

You have two choices. Either tell her how to make, chain, beam, thread, sley, and tie on a new warp, or you do it.

You may not believe it, but the latter is quicker. Make *her* bring the loom to *you*, and leave it for a few days. You do some simple math on paper for yourself. There are blank dents in the (usually) wooden or plastic reed. There are blank string heddles on the (usually) two harnesses. And it won't be enough, I can almost promise. Take the total dents number and tie string heddles to make enough, making very sure your jig is correct, not one you have used for other string heddles. You will probably have to make one for this job, using one of the string heddles off the little loom. When you come to put them on the loom, you will probably find the harnesses fastened to the top and bottom bars with tapes that do not permit the full width of the reed to be used.

Get some good soft cord and make four knotted loops to replace the tapes and proceed to replace in a way that uses the full width of the heddle bars, which are a European loom's equivalent of harness frames. Then you make a long, fairly coarse warp, preferably in bright color(s), beam it, thread it, sley it, and tie it on. Voila! The loom is ready for the child, and it is time to call the mother and tell her she may pick it up.

The mother will want to pay you "something for your trouble—just to make me feel better." There is a lovely way to get off the hook that won't embarrass either of you. Just tell her this time the warp is on you, but next time you will "help" her do it, and let her pay for the materials from then on.

One of two things will happen. You will never hear from her again because the child has found it's not much fun if he/she can order up new warps and they just appear. Or, you will get another call in about a week—maybe two weeks if flu is going around—to say "we've run out of warp again." In that case, you invite the lady over for lunch and the two of you make a warp and put it on. And if the child is ten or older, you bypass the mother and invite the child over for lunch. Children are not given enough credit for a lot of things nowadays, and a child of ten can be taught weaving with no trouble, strain, or tears; a great deal of pleasure is there for him/her to discover if the opportunity is found.

Church Fair Demonstrations and What to Take

A request for an outdoor weaving demonstration at a church summer fair is another type of phone call you will eventually get. And the church does not even have to be your own denomination. If you say yes and have a table loom only, make sure they give you a table. Elementary logic, but church fair ladies are not unfailingly logical.

And don't wind all your bobbins ahead of time, unless you have only an electric bobbin winder. Screw the manual winder to your loom and do some bobbins while you are demonstrating. Make your pattern simple, so you can chatter and answer questions while weaving.

If you can let people try out the weaving process, your immediate area will be very popular indeed. And that goes for adults as well as children. You could take along some things you have woven, scarves, cases for sunglasses, place mats—things like that. One of my young weaving friends makes impressive pocket money by picking up orders at church fairs. Potential customers put their name, phone number, address, items wanted, in what colors, and their price range into her little notebook. Though she is far too attractive to be so well organized, she does very well indeed with this soft-sell approach.

Check for Poison Ivy. If you are taking a floor loom to demonstrate on, try to get them to give you a piece of plywood to put under it. Maybe it's only rocky New England greensward where there are bumps under the treadles, no matter where you move, but I have met up with poison ivy there too, and you will probably be weaving barefoot.

Another Push to Find the Nearest Craft Center

The sooner you get familiar with your local craft centers and weavers guilds the better. But I do warn you, you will get a telephone call in the middle of your favorite TV program, and the person will be new to the area, wanting to learn to weave or to join a guild, or just talk weaving.

Most guilds and centers I know have little brochures you can take a small stack of and pack neatly into your handbag. Drop a couple off at the neighborhood yarn or embroidery shops, and they will probably be pleased too.

Being Helpful Is Really Quite Easy

Being a good neighbor sounds time consuming, but in the long run— say a year—it doesn't take very long. And who knows how much good you have done? Besides didn't someone help you at the beginning?

19.
Joining a Guild

Joining a guild is easy, just pay dues. Finding a guild to join is the difficult part for many of us. If you are a new weaver who has learned from books only, then you don't know any weavers, so we must discover other sources for you to ask.

How to Find One
Do you have a craft center near your town? If you do not, try the library bulletin board because they may post booklets from one in your general area. Then call that craft center and ask them your questions.

Check weaving books in the library too. They may contain a guild address because some books are privately printed or mimeographed.

Look for weavers at church fairs. If it is not church fair season, find the name of the church fair manager. She/he may know of a weaver. These days it is reasonably safe to say—scratch a weaver and you will find a guild.

Go to craft shows. If there is no weaving there, ask a potter if he/she knows any weavers.

Or call your local hospital to see if they know any weavers who would know of a guild.

Your local little craft shop may have handwoven merchandise. Ask who made it and where they might live. It may take a while, but keep at it.

I have saved the best for last. If you have moved into a town absolutely cold and must find a weavers guild before you find a good butcher or an acceptable nursery school, get in touch with The Handweavers Guild of America. They will have somebody write and tell you where and when the next guild meeting in your state is. How is that for kindness from a nationwide network of volunteers?

How to Get a Lot Out of One
When you find a guild, do join, even if you are not a joining type of person. The rewards of belonging to a guild are many.

You meet like-minded people, and therefore have conversational opportunities. Whether a weaver has been weaving five months or five decades, he or she can generally answer your question—though it is often by introducing you to someone else who knows more about the subject.

Guilds have libraries—some are excellent, some are good, some are poor. As with any other book, a weaving book is new to you if you have not read it.

Because our state guild meets five times a year only, that means you may borrow a book two months at a minimum, and four months if you take it out in May, since there is no meeting until September. No charge if you bring it back on time. And no other library I ever heard of can match that deal.

One of the most useful things a guild does is hold meetings on subjects that are of absolutely no interest to you at all.

Suppose you are a modern wall hangings person who doesn't have the inclination to make anything as useful as even a bookmark. Do take my advice, and go to the lecture and slide show on colonial textiles. Out of that time spent may come a whole new range of wall hangings. Or you might help your best friend, the colonial house lady, who needs to know what kind of living room curtains to put up in her 1721 saltbox.

I went to a guild lecture on spinning a few years ago, in spite of my limited interest in the subject. So far, it has cost me two spinning wheels; books; carders; fleeces from Ireland, Connecticut, and Scotland; a niddy noddy; and a couple of workshops when I could get them. Fascinating. And once you have used a bit of handspun wool in a project, the bet about eating only one peanut becomes one you will understand perfectly.

As I mentioned a few chapters back, guilds also have workshops on different subjects at different times of the year. They hire an expert to teach and you pay a low amount to attend. Try out one you're not particularly drawn to.

Do you want to know quite a bit about tapestry and its possibilities beyond the basic directions? Then go to a tapestry workshop when the opportunity arises. This holds true even if you don't anticipate having time to do much tapestry in the next year. Catch the lessons when you can. And please be prepared to have somebody at the loom to your left interested in making Christmas bells, while the loom to your right is churning out samples that will be used to make fine linen or silk and gold ecclesiastical vestments.

Don't be surprised either if the ecclesiastical vestment loom is operated by an earnest and lovely lass, wearing sandals she has made herself, and a jeans outfit she has embroidered herself.

With a learned skill, infinite variations in application are possible, and weavers turn out to be most inventive.

How to Help Your Guild

There are chores to do and committees to be active on in any guild I know of. No matter how green you are at weaving, there is always some contribution you can make for a year or so—even if it just involves making a pound cake for every meeting in the year.

Guilds, like other volunteer organizations, thrive only with the contributions of members. This means your time as well as your dues. It doesn't matter in what physical shape you are, even house-bound, you can do something—mend library books, re-cover the mimeographed booklets, straighten out the samples file.

Join a guild! When you need three ounces of purple Swedish linen two weeks before Easter, you too may have a friend from whom you can borrow. And you must admit there are more conversational possibilities inherent in that loan than borrowing a cup of sugar.

20.

Where Do You Go From Here?

Of course you don't know everything about weaving yet. And because there is so much to learn, you probably never will know everything. At this point, you don't really know how to do all the things I have covered in this book since a lot of the processes should be done a few times to fix the principles in your mind.

Have Confidence!

I trust that you have a certain amount of confidence in your own common sense and its ability to solve problems by thinking before you actually *do* anything. You now know a lot more than a good percentage of weavers, and you should be aware of this.

If you see a weaving you wish to duplicate, find the threading, tie-up, and treadling, make and beam the warp for it so you are satisfied with the result, then thread, sley, tie on evenly, and weave it off. Well, you have come a long way.

Building Individuality

And if you see a weaving you like and can adapt it from the given draft to conform to your own notions of color, materials, sley, and pattern changes, you are even farther along the road.

A subscription to one of the weaving bulletins mentioned in an earlier chapter will add a lot to your weaving life—not because you will wish to copy the samples from each issue; not at all. You should not take the colors or materials those samples are done in as indications of the weaver's taste. There may have been a great amount of yarn on his/her shelves, and the sample was seen as a good chance to make more storage space. You may say to yourself, "I don't like the color, materials, or function, but I do like the technique. Plus I was looking for a way to use that handspun gray wool in a scarf."

If you choose to make a gray handspun wool scarf out of a pattern designed for draperies, then there will be certain changes you will have to make—but look at the fun and the learning that will occur while you are making those changes.

You can look up craft shows in your immediate area and put reminders on the family calendar. Some of the showings will be astonishingly good, and some will be awful. There is one advantage to an awful craft show that may not have entered your head. You will see that you know more than you had realized. This is not a thought to make you puff up with pride, but rather to make you go on to the next plateau with more confidence—more justified confidence—than you previously had.

You can take one short course a year if your budget is tight. It doesn't have to be a summer abroad at a craft center either; it can be a four day workshop ten miles from home or school.

Problems in Workshops

Because I have a friend who has had troubles in workshops, and because I have been both a weaving teacher and a student, let me offer some advice on how to cope with various problems you may encounter.

As a teacher I tell my students, "If you don't know—ask." If I am busy, they should stand by me until I notice them.

After all, if I am helping someone else, it is not a private matter—I am not a marriage counsellor or a financial advisor. The topic in these classes is weaving—some aspect of weaving.

I have no objection if someone stands by me—with no particular problem—merely listening to what I have to say about the other person's weaving problem. Because I have set up the situation myself, I know that someone standing by me is likely to have a problem. This way I can say, "I'll be over to your loom in just a minute."

If there is suddenly a line up of four or five students, I can fairly judge I have not made a point clear. I can ask the first person what the problem is, restate it loudly enough so all can hear, ask if anyone else has the same problem and, if there are several assents, say I'll be over to the blackboard or a loom very shortly.

Of Good Teachers and Poor Teachers and Certain Students

From a weaving student's point of view, you must accept that things have not changed all that much since your own school days. There are good teachers, and there certainly are poor ones. Is it a new thought that you can often get at least as much information out of the poor teachers?

Being a poor teacher does not mean that you are not knowledgeable. It can just as easily mean you have difficulty communicating your knowledge, can't think up a simple way to show some process, or are afraid of the students.

If you find yourself in a class where you feel the loudest student is getting all the attention, or you have asked a question and it has not been answered, or the teacher promised to come to your loom after lunch, but did not, then go to the teacher and say you need a minute when it is your turn. This is not being abrasive or pushy. You have paid good money to take this course. You are as entitled as the next student to get your questions answered and to receive value for your tuition.

Teachers are like waiters in some ways. A good waiter will come into the dining room and realize there is a problem. A very good waiter will know immediately that table three needs more water. An excellent waiter will know, almost instinctively that the corner table has been waiting for attention too long and is seething, even though they are smiling and conversing pleasantly.

Well, let's face it—all teachers are not excellent waiters, or even good ones. So relax and try to get the most you can out of that class. You paid your money, and nobody is going to be very sympathetic if you say at the end of the course that you didn't get what you wanted, because you couldn't get the teacher's attention. I know I wouldn't be.

How to Win In a Losing Situation
The previous situation is not at all to be confused with having registered for the wrong course—either your fault or the craft center's—where you are not going to get what you want, no matter what you do.

Supposing it is an intermediate tapestry workshop, but the majority of the students are brand new weavers who have to be taught how to make warps—on your time and money. I would be tempted to go to the craft center office and discuss this with them.

If you are "stuck" in the class because you have paid for your motel room and the family will pick you up Friday night, you have an entirely different situation to deal with.

You can get what you are able to out of the course, read all the weaving books in their library, make the complaining visit to the office and see what they have to suggest, put up with the situation and see what you can learn from it, or just simmer the week away in black fury. I recommend any or all actions except the last one.

Non-Weaving Activities
When your free time at home is not enough to make a warp, or your threads order has not come in yet—you can always reread your weaving books. Supposing you have three or four books, and have had no occasion to want to do embroidery weaves. You might check all the references to embroidery weaves in all the books you have, purely as an intellectual exercise. If you do not enjoy this type of activity, for heaven's sake don't do it again. There is the type of mind that only wishes to solve immediate problems, and there is nothing wrong with minds like that.

If you like patterns for themselves, why not play with graph paper and colored pencils on a plane or bus trip?

If you are a museum-goer, the next time you visit you could ask what they have in textiles. If you are off on vacation, either here or abroad, be sure to check local museums, as well as craft or souvenir shops, to see what they have in textiles. Book shops these days usually have at least some weaving books to flip through, when you have the time. And don't scorn the little paperback translations with Scandinavian titles. Some are exceptionally good.

The point I am making is you do not have to have a threaded loom in front of you to learn more about weaving or to gain pleasure from the hobby.

This craft can be very expensive, but it need not be at all. Cheap threads, using complicated techniques, can be as much fun and at least as impressive as very simple techniques using horrendously expensive threads. Regardless of the techniques or uses of the end product, I am not an advocate of long warps for beginners. I do believe that the practice of putting on several short ones makes for an assurance that is well worth the extra time spent.

Cutting Off a Warp That You Want to Put Back Later On
While we are on the subject of long or short warps, there will come the time when you have warp on for eight place mats, have only three woven, own just one loom, and urgently want to make a scarf for a birthday present.

There is a perfectly simple way to do this that requires cutting off the place mat warp, but in such a way that it can be put back on the loom and rethreaded.

Read the following instructions through before you do anything with the loom, except perhaps to dust it. The only absolute requirement is to put the cross back in before you cut the warp threads.

The easiest routine I know is the following. If you are making place mats, allow enough unwoven warp at the front of the last pick of weaving to use as fringe. Smear some white glue from selvedge to selvedge on the cloth at the fell—where the warp becomes cloth. Let it dry completely. If they are not to be fringed, the glue will go on what eventually becomes part of the hem.

Now get out thé lease sticks and treadle 13. Put one stick in behind the harnesses, into the shed that you have made this way. Shove that stick as far back toward the back beam as you can. Treadle 24 and put in the other lease stick. It will be in the new shed you have made and will also go in behind the harnesses. Shove the second lease stick as far back as you can. Tie the two sticks together, as you did when you were first making the warp a few place mats ago.

Now go to the front of the loom, loosen the tension a little, and cut the warp between the fringe allowance and the beater. Slip knot it immediately so you won't lose the cross you methodically replaced. Unroll the warp, either through the heddles (which I feel wears the ends unnecessarily) or over the top castle.

If you choose the latter method, you must unsley and unthread the ends in groups before you slip knot them. Keep unwinding the warp,

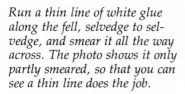

Run a thin line of white glue along the fell, selvedge to selvedge, and smear it all the way across. The photo shows it only partly smeared, so that you can see a thin line does the job.

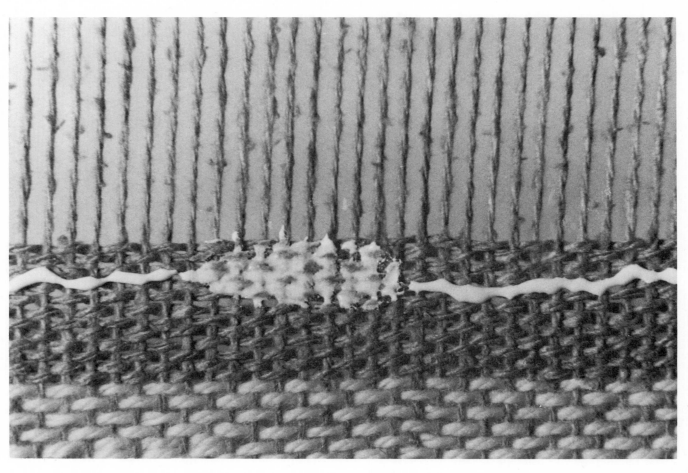

pushing the lease sticks toward the back beam as you unwind. Then put a string through the cross—exactly as you did before you took the warp off the warping frame. This will leave your lease sticks free for the new warp you are about to make.

Run a long cord through the row of warp loops on the back bar. It will go exactly the same path as the back bar and will be knotted to form a big loop. If you do this, nothing dire can happen when you go to the front of the warp. Now hold on at the slip knots, with enough tension so the warp does not droop, and snap it lightly a couple of times to reorder it properly before you chain it.

It is still attached at the back of the loom, and if the three cords have—by any very remote chance—popped off and thus permitted the back bar to crash to the floor, you still have that loose cord loop in, so you can put the warp back on the bar and then go back to tie choke ties.

I like a few choke ties sprinkled through a warp, and it is possible even in a case like this. True, they are more difficult to place correctly than when a warp is still on a frame or mill. But here is one more situation where not quite right is far better than nothing. If you can find someone to hold the slip knotted front of the warp while you do the choke ties, it will be easier.

Then chain the warp carefully, put it into a bag so that the warp threads won't catch on anything, label it—ends per inch, threading, tie up, and treadling—then put it away until you finish the birthday present. When you put it back on, treat it just like a new warp. But make sure you have the extra inches for tying on at the front of the warp before you cut it off in the first place.

Most people put on extra inches when they wind a warp, but—I emphasize, I repeat, I implore—be very sure you did before you go and cut that warp.

You may prefer to sally forth to the marts of trade and buy a scarf, rather than end up with a short place mat because you did not allow enough extra inches when you wound the place mat warp.

When you have your place mats off the loom, and before you wash them, run a row of zig zag stitches on the sewing machine at the fell; or a couple of rows of fine stitches if your machine does not zig zag. Either of these stitching systems will probably go into the glued area, and eventually the hem, so it is perfectly all right.

Cutting Off a Warp Because the Weaving Is Finished

Now this is a lot simpler than the previous procedure, but there are certain steps that will make it even easier.

First, make very sure the weaving is finished. Is it long enough? Have you ended with a completion of a certain treadling sequence—if that is what you wanted to do? Have you allowed for shrinkage? And for warp take up?

Now sit and look at the warp for a few minutes, while going over in your mind what you are proposing to do. Should the project be a scarf, you want warp ends cut long enough to make a fringe. Slightly loosen the loom tension at the back, so that when you cut the warps they will not—celebrating their release from tension—jump and tangle with each other.

If you are at the end of the warp, it could mean cutting the warp right at the back bar. Far better to cut off fringe later on than to wish you had it to cut.

Treadle 13 and put a lease stick behind the harnesses, into the resulting shed. Then shove it close to the back beam. Treadle 24 and put the second lease stick back into that shed. Shove it far back. The photo shows the sticks in place, before they are tied together. Make them parallel and tie them together.

Cut the warp in sections between the beater and the fringe allowance. After each cut, slip knot the warp immediately to prevent losing the cross. Loosely overhand knot the fringe to keep the weft from moving out of place.

Top Left
A few choke ties are good for any warp, and you can even do them on this one. However, if another person holds the slip knotted front of the warp while you tie, it will be easier.

Bottom Left
A cord has been run through the line of loops on the back bar, duplicating the path of the back bar, then knotted. Use another length of the cord to make a loop in the cross where the lease sticks are, because you can't put a warp containing lease sticks into a little plastic bag. If you will check your warp before you put it into the bag you should find it has choke ties throughout, slip knots at the front, a tie at the cross, and a loop at the back.

Top Right
Here is the way you start to chain a warp. That goes for any warp. Obviously the one used for the photograph is not the one just cut off the loom, because the front ends are looped—as they come off the warping frame—not slip knotted as they come off the loom.

Bottom Right
Here is a warp all chained and ready to go on a loom, or into a plastic bag until the time you want to beam it. The counting tie is very clear right at the cross and the light colored loop to its left is part of the loop tying the cross. At the right of the warp, just before the end, a knot of one of the choke ties is only just visible.

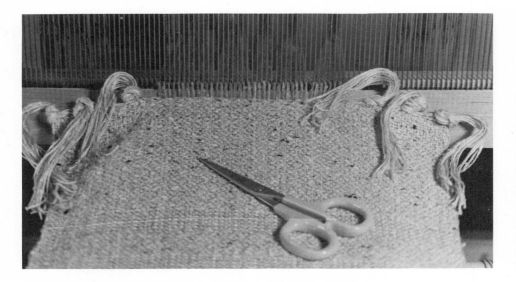

Cut a half inch of warps at right or left selvedge, pull toward you (also out from the heddles and reed if you cut at the back bar) then immediately overhand knot (loosely) to keep the weft in place. Keep cutting and knotting, going toward the center from each side. These loose knots will be undone later on, when you have decided exactly the number of ends you want in each knot of fringe.

This picture is really ridiculous when you fully understand it. The top (apparently white) loops are the warp on the back bar. You are looking directly down at the four metal harnesses of this loom. Lying on the material—a pure silk scarf made of leftovers—are two shuttles. The boat shuttle was used until it would not go through the shed any more, since the back bar had been advanced too close to the heddles. The stick shuttle was wound with weft silk and used to gain the two and a half inches (6.4 cm) needed to finish the scarf. Not a practice I recommend, but it did solve the problem, and the scarf looked beautiful after it was washed.

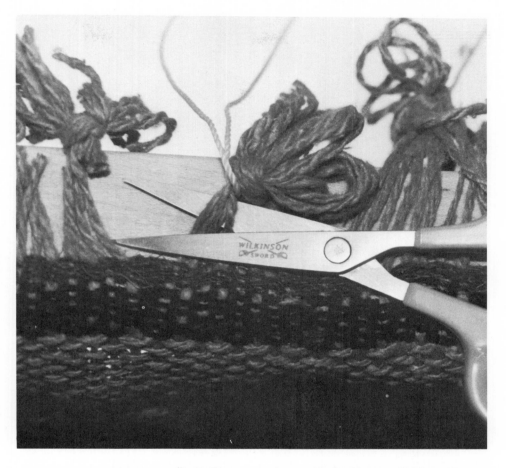

This sample did not work out, so it is being cut off the loom before the warp is resleyed for another one. Use the cutting technique only if you don't want fringe on the project—after smearing white glue at the fell. Notice the slip knots into which you lashed the nylon cords and are now inserting the scissors. If you do want fringe, then don't cut these knots. Unslip knot them to get the project separated from the loom, and immediately loosely overhand knot the bundles.

Here the job of picking out starter weft and tying fringe for the silk scarf is in progress. Use sharp pointed scissors and do the job by small numbers of ends. Because this was a fine closely set warp, the fringe knots are tied every half inch and will be adjusted until they are in a precise row. Then the last tug on each knot will be given, at the same time as the knot is pushed toward the fell.

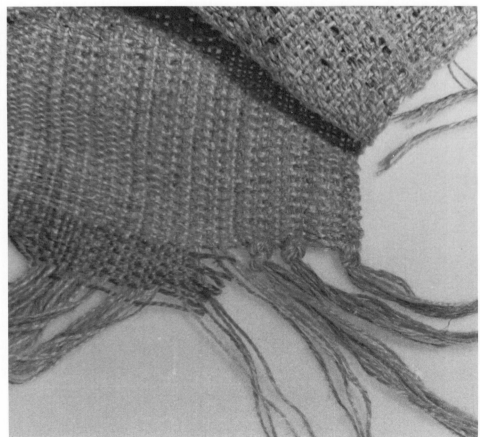

Cut ½" (1.3 cm) of selvedge warps at right or left, and pull forward the cut ends from the reed and heddles. Overhand knot as close to the fell as you can, but loosely. You will want to untie this step later on to do a certain number of ends, perhaps in a certain knot. Right now you are just knotting warp ends so that the wefts won't slip out of place. And they will if you skip this step.

Cut and tie the selvedge half inch on the opposite side in the same manner. Now cut and tie in inch groups for a few inches going toward the center; then change to the other side to cut and tie a few more inches. Finish with the center inches.

The next step is to completely release the front tension. Unroll your project carefully until you get to where you slip knotted the warp ends at the front, before you laced them to the front bar. Unlace the nylon cord, which will separate the woven project from the loom.

Finish it as you will, perhaps macrame, perhaps wash and press, perhaps steam and press. It all depends on what you have woven. But do remember to take time to feel pleasure at the job you have done. This is a hobby and hobbies are to be enjoyed.

There are other ways to cut off the loom, depending on what the current project is. Should it be yard goods, or a fine runner, you run a line of white glue (as was recommended for the mats in the previous section) from selvedge to selvedge, over the last ¼" (.64 cm) or so of the woven part. Again, smear and be sure to let it dry completely. Then cut the warps. This gluing is only for a project that is to be washed as part of the finishing process, bearing in mind that white glue washes out with soap and water. Before you wash it, remember to run a line of zigzag stitch on the sewing machine—as you did for the mats—close to the fell.

And where do you go from here, now that your loom is empty? To the next project, of course.

The End—and The Beginning

No, these are not final words of wisdom, "recipes," or little hints I forgot to put into their proper chapters—nothing at all like that.

This is the part where I repeat what I have been saying all along. You are doing very well. You can now weave, perhaps not as easily as I can, perhaps more easily—who knows?

You have started along the road of weaving, and I hope I have prevented some worries, solved some problems, and given you the confidence you have fairly earned.

There are more books to be read—and written—and enjoyed. There are more good warps to be made—and poor ones as well. There are more successful projects to be woven—and some you would prefer to forget. Both types are learning experiences, as current jargon has it.

There are more people to be shown weaving, and to enjoy weaving, and to learn weaving. If you are fortunate, you will be a part of this.

Whether weaving becomes your way of life, or a pleasing occasional hobby, all weavers will always wish you well—including this one . . . .

Bibliography

Atwater, M.M. *Byways in Handweaving*. New York: Macmillan, 1968

Birrell, Verla. *The Textile Arts*. New York: Schocken Books, 1973

Black, Mary E. *New Key to Weaving*. New York: Macmillan, 1961

Chamberlain, Marcia, and Crockett, Candace. *Beyond Weaving*. New York: Watson-Guptill, 1974; London: Pitman Publishing, 1974

Collingwood, Peter. *The Techniques of Rug Weaving*. New York: Watson-Guptill, 1969; London: Faber and Faber, 1968

Davison, Marguerite P. *A Handweavers Pattern Book*. Swarthmore, Pa.: Marguerite P. Davison, 1944

Emery, Irene. *The Primary Structure of Fabrics*. Washington, D.C.: The Textile Museum, 1966

Frey, Berta. *Designing and Drafting for Handweavers*. New York: Macmillan, 1975

Halsey, Mike, and Youngman, Lore. *Foundations of Weaving*. New York: Watson-Guptill, 1975

Regensteiner, Else. *The Art of Weaving*. New York: Van Nostrand Reinhold, 1970; London: Studio Vista

Weigle, Palmy. *Color Exercises for the Weaver*. New York: Watson-Guptill, 1976

Znamierowski, Nel. *Weaving, Step-by-Step*. New York: Golden Press, 1967; London: Pan

Index

Edited by Donna Wilkinson
Designed by Jay Anning